Carole Marsh's CAREERS CURRICULUM™

MIDDLE SCHOOL
HIGH SCHOOL
COLLEGE & BEYOND

JOB TRACKS: 60* Great Careers

and How to Get from Where You Are... to Where You Want to Go!

CAROLE MARSH

*Real job success stories from 21st century career pathways!

Editor:	Janice Baker
Assistant Editors:	Charles Peterson
	Madeline Vogler
	Adrianna Atkinson
Cover Design:	Lisa Kelly
Content Design:	Randolyn Friedlander
	Lisa Kelly
	Maggie Bowers
Project Manager:	Paige Muh

For additional information about Carole Marsh's Careers Curriculum or other curriculum products, contact:

Gallopade International
P.O. Box 2779
Peachtree City, Georgia 30269
800-536-2438, ext. 11
www.careerscurriculum.com
www.gallopade.com

Carole Marsh's CAREERS CURRICULUM™

Books

Essential Skills for the Real World of Work: Things *Every* Student Must Know!

Job Tracks: 60* Great Careers—and How to Get from Where You Are...to Where You Want to Go! *Real Job Success Stories from 21st Century Career Pathways!

Would *You* Hire This Person?: A Look at Getting Hired (or Not!)... from the Point of View of Your (Possible!) Future Employer

The Parent and Teacher's Guide to Helping Students Navigate the Bumpy Road from School to More School, First Job, and Career

Business Ethics and Etiquette for Students— You MUST Know These!

WORK WORDS: Job/Business/Career Words and Terms You Need to Know!

Also available in ebook formats

People don't quit JOBS they love.— John Ralston, former NFL coach

Contents

A Word from the Author

Whether you call your trek from school to job a pathway, a track, or something else, it WILL be an adventure, and I wish you well!

In this book, you'll see two kinds of pages:

1. The success stories of young men and women just a tad older than you. I thought telling their story "backwards"—what they're doing (and making, as in $, $$, or $$$!) now, how they got there, and especially what they might have done differently, if anything, would be helpful to you. Lots of jobs, lots of choices!

2. Pages of tips that I wish someone had told me "way back when" I was your age and trying to find my path, my track to the future. It was NOT a straight line, I can tell you that!

Most of all, I hope this book is encouraging! There are not so many rules, you know? Education is important, often essential, but so is experience, and many other things—as you'll learn—on the road from school to more school and/or school to job-readiness.

I think you'll learn a lot of "between the lines" subtleties and nuances that often take many adults years to learn. Hey, I want to give you a fast track, so all these "insider secrets" are included—read em and reap!

Don't forget to have fun on your journey; you only get to do it once! We are all out here cheering you on and waiting for you—there's lots of work to be done. I promise!

Carole Marsh, CEO
Gallopade International
Peachtree City, Georgia

Desire! That's the one secret of every man's CAREER. Not education. Not being born with hidden talent. Desire.—Bobby Unser

Job Title: Agricultural Scientist

Success

Why did I become an agricultural scientist? Because I enjoy working with the environment. On a daily basis, I help farmers across America maintain the quality of our nation's food supply— that's food for grocery stores, restaurants, fast food chains, and your grandma's home cooking. An added bonus is that I often do field work and get to operate heavy machinery. It's not all sitting behind a microscope and splicing genes.

Cool Stuff

Did you know that carrots weren't always orange? Or that without ag scientists we'd never be able to feed all 300 million U.S. citizens? I'm satisfied knowing that my job is crucial, besides occasionally feeling like a mad scientist with test tubes and microscopes. It's not my specialty area, but one of my colleagues is working with nanotechnology to detect food contaminants!

Skills

I loved biology and chemistry in high school, but didn't want to be locked in a laboratory all my life. Ag science lets me get out in the open air and talk with real people. Good communication is essential, and an interest in the environment is a great start. Maybe you want to sharpen up your analytical and problem solving skills. Saving the environment AND keeping our economy going is a daunting challenge.

Education

This field requires a college degree, and many of my coworkers specialized with a Ph.D. I was a neo-hippie in high school and almost dropped out to pursue my psychedelic art career. My parents forced me into a community college where I took an environmentalism course that changed my life. I had always wanted to conserve the environment but just didn't know how. Turns out it was easier than I thought and more rewarding.

Financial Factor

Don't believe in buried treasure? The gold is in the soil, you just have to look through a microscope. Agricultural Science isn't a poor man's field. I average $55,000 per year. It may be true, the family farm is dying out, but the opportunities for graduates in the food, agriculture, and environmental sciences are in demand now! (There are more jobs out there right now than there are people to fill them.) Clothing trends come and go, but breakfast, lunch, and dinner never go out of fashion.

If I Could Go Back

I would have gotten my act together sooner. I still have time for my art, but I should have taken that AP biology course my senior year. And believe it or not, I would have taken a business class or joined Future Business Leaders of America. Farmers need as much advice about their businesses as they do about crops. Now that I have the money, I will "go back" sometime soon and get my Ph.D.

The Role of Failure in Success

You ARE going to fail. Probably many times. Get over it. These people did. Most successful people have similar stories!

He was born poor. He was barely educated. He lost his job. He failed at his first run for office. He failed as a businessperson. He failed as a farmer. His girlfriend died. He had a nervous breakdown. He was defeated in another election. And again. And again. And again. And again. And again. And yet again.

Then Abraham Lincoln was elected president.

He missed more than 9,000 shots. He lost almost 300 games. In 26 games, he missed the winning shot. He was a total failure. That's why he succeeded.

He is Michael Jordan.

He failed at every single business he tried.

Then Milton Hershey invented milk chocolate, a company, a town, a famous orphanage, and made a lot of people happy in the process.

These three dingbats dropped out of college. They built a new kind of machine: the computer.

You might recognize their names: Steve Jobs, Bill Gates, Michael Dell

No is just a stepping stone to Yes — KEEP WALKING!

Job Title: Chef

Success

I live to cook, and I cook to live. It's a delicious circle that pays my bills too. Four days a week, I work in a mansion for a family of six and in a small apartment for a busy working couple. On the weekends, I'm a chef at a 4-star restaurant to keep my skills on the cutting edge of cuisine. Shopping for ingredients is half the fun, but what I love most is getting to know the clients. Everybody has unique taste buds! No lie, sometimes it's about making money, but flexibility is my game. My business partner and I started a small catering company, and we're always up for a new challenge. Vegan? I know how to make meatless masterpieces. Home cooking? I learned my father's secrets. Food art? I want my culinary palette to delight your palate… creativity is only second to flavor.

Cool Stuff

The average 70-year-old has spent about 6 years of his or her life eating. Whether in the house or at the restaurant, food-preparers are always welcome. Why not be the best and get paid? I always wanted a sword, but my mother said she didn't want a one-eyed son or injured cat. Now I play with the sharpest knives available. I consider everything you can eat as a part of my arsenal. From basic pasta dishes to marinated eel, quality ingredients go a long way, and sugar and spice make everything nice.

Skills

Experience in the kitchen is invaluable. You need to be resourceful, independent, and have good taste (literally!). General knowledge of kitchen hygiene will guarantee no lost appetites. Communication, friendliness, and honesty will get you the job faster than your cooking. Keep in mind families will invite only trustworthy private chefs into their homes. Take business classes, because cooking is a growing industry where a smart entrepreneur can make a pretty penny.

Education

No degree required, but to get anywhere, you'll need to attend a vocational cooking school, a culinary institute, or a college degree program. Lasting a few months to 2 years or more, culinary school teaches advanced techniques, international cuisine, and cooking styles! Experience is best, so start early. I got a job as a line cook in high school and knew there was so much more to cooking. Really, it's all about practice until perfect, which means making inedible mistakes along the way.

Financial Factor

Starting salary for a personal or private chef can be around $20,000, but it depends on where you live. Working regularly for a restaurant and doing private cooking on the side can raise your salary to around $35,000. Big cities are better, providing a wealthier client base and busier people who don't have time to cook. A good private chef in a large city like New York can earn between $40,000 and $70,000 a year!

If I Could Go Back

I would spend more time with my grandmother, learning how to make her Hungarian Goulash! Some of the best cooking advice I picked up at home and then developed in school and finally mastered in my career. I'm always experimenting and learning, but a solid foundation is priceless. It's never too late to be adventurous. Try all different foods, so that your mouth knows the difference between "mmmmm" and "eh."

It Was Just an Internship...

Emily is my piano teacher's daughter. She graduated from high school and it was the summer before she started college. She wanted some "real work experience" so she came to my company to intern for free for a couple of months.

We were starting a series on the Civil War and I put Emily on writing a timeline of the war, a timeline of African American history, and calculating the amount of blood shed during the four-year war.

She brought her own laptop and lunch and pitched right in. Emily did a great job. She had initiative, even contacted the CDC to see how much blood various types of wounds produced. She bought a book she found about animals in the war and wrote up all the facts; we used those too. I would have hired Emily, but...

She went to her first day of college, planning on a degree in music. The first day of class she had to stand up and sing. The head of the music department was there and pulled her out of freshman class and sent her to senior class (for singing, anyway) so she could star in the annual school musical. She was that good; she got a Nashville recording contract to do songs for a new kind of Christmas card/CD combo.

A big recording studio that represents Grammy winners asked Emily to intern with them, then work part time. She brought coffee, made copies, and soon began to arrange tours for groups like Lady Antebellum. The company offered her a full time job. Emily switched to night school, changed her major to music management, and took the job.

Emily ended up with a full scholarship, a job traveling around the nation (and to the music award shows), and continued her own performing.

When I congratulated Emily on all her success, she modestly said, "Thank you for letting me work that summer. It gave me confidence to learn a little about how a real business operates."

Emily was 19.

You gotta get out there. You gotta show up.

I don't talk to Emily much anymore. I think she's in London. But I do hear her on the radio!

Job Title: Aircraft Mechanic

Success

I love the routine of not having a routine. As a mechanic who works on airplanes, I have to know about the entire airplane, including the airframe—the body of the plane, including the wings, the tail, and the fuselage—and the powerplant—the engine or engines. Sometimes I do major repairs and sometimes I do minor repairs on the fly! What I really like about my job is that I get to use my mind and my hands, and I don't have to stay in one place too long. I get to figure out why things work (or don't) and then fix them

Cool Tools

I have many highly specialized tools just for working on airplanes. I use a micrometer, which measures aircraft parts to .001 (that's one one-thousandth!) of an inch. In my shop, I lift planes using giant hydraulic jacks so that I can change tires and inspect landing gear. I troubleshoot electrical problems using the latest, greatest computerized tools. The really cool tool? A four-foot-long wrench! Where else could you use one of those?

Skills

If you like to work with your hands, don't mind getting a little dirty (sometimes), and like the idea of not having a "regular" day, this might be the job for you. I have to be precise and pay attention to every detail, and I get to use my problem-solving skills almost all the time.

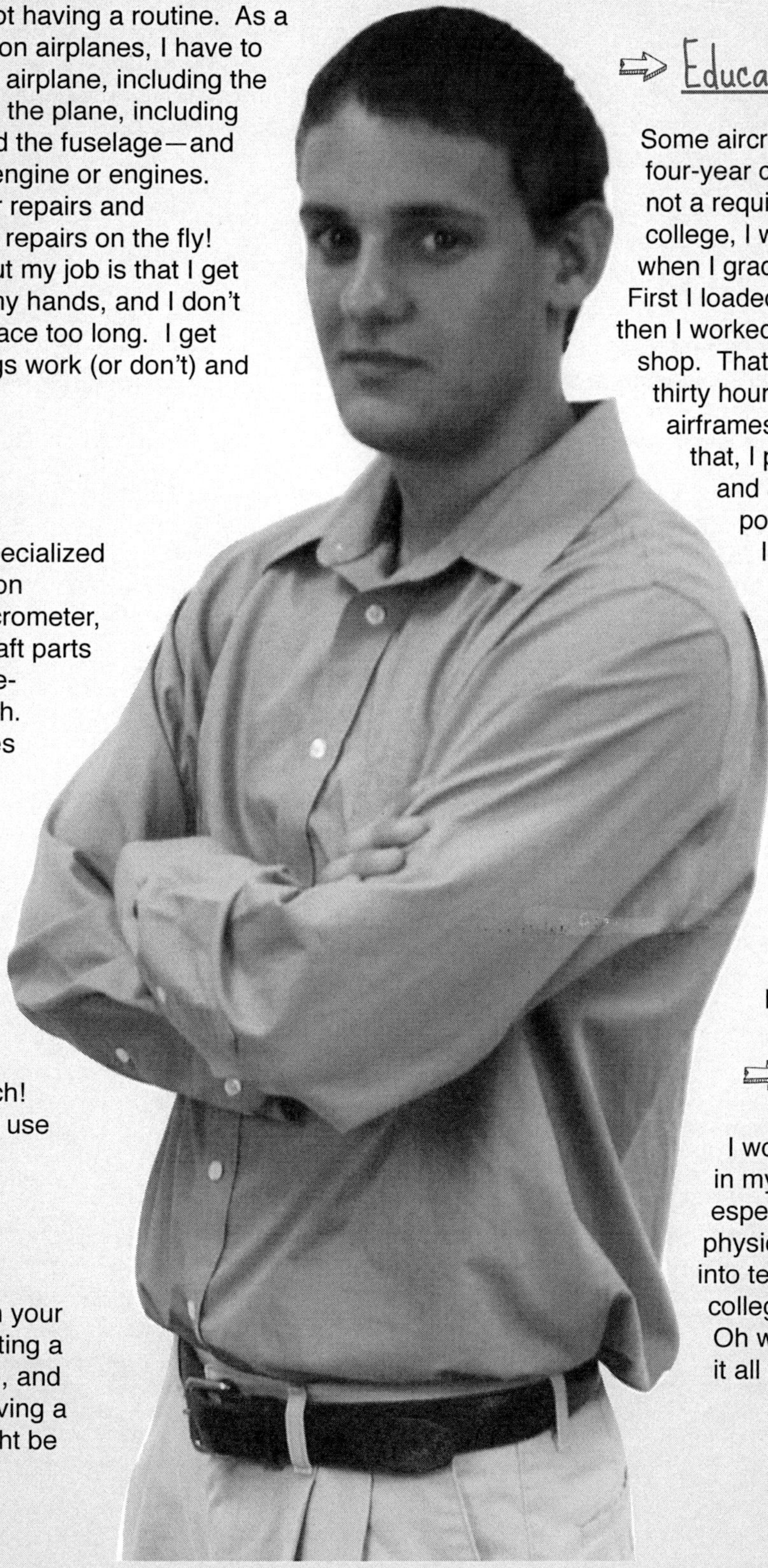

Education

Some aircraft mechanics have two- or four-year college degrees, but that's not a requirement. To earn money for college, I went to work for a major airline when I graduated from high school. First I loaded luggage onto planes, and then I worked my way into a maintenance shop. That's where I gained the required thirty hours of experience working on airframes and powerplants. After that, I passed the tests required and applied for my airframe and power plant (A&P) licenses. If I couldn't have gotten into the maintenance shop, I could've gone to technical school for about two years instead.

Financial Factor

Aircraft mechanics make good money, about $76,000/year, and I maximized my earning potential by getting the A&P rating for both airframes and powerplants.

If I Could Go Back

I would have paid extra attention in my high school science classes, especially physical science and physics, and I would have looked into technical school (instead of college) right out of high school. Oh well! I lived and I learned and it all worked out.

Some Things You Just Gotta Do... If You Want to Get Ahead Vs. Behind

You have to go out: An old Coast Guard motto is "You don't have to come back...you just have to go out." Get your guts on. Sitting in school is the easy part; now you gotta get out there.

Just show up: It may be total failure, a waste of time, the chance of a lifetime, or just fun. You will never know unless you show up.

Failure is good: If you fail, you learn that "that didn't work that way at that time." That's all failure, a stepping stone to success, is. Get back on the horse, or back in the batting line, or whatever...but keep moving.

Success does not come to the wimpy: The only way you can be the last person standing is to stand there and keep standing.

Roll with the punches: Be resilient. Get comfortable outside of your comfort zone. You'll soon find you're pretty good at handling anything thrown at you—maybe even enjoy it.

Act confident: ...even when you're not. You might not fool your boss, but you might fool yourself. Pretend, fake it, and soon you may discover you're a lot more confident than you were. Confidence begets confidence.

Believe: If you don't believe in yourself, your talents, your willingness, your abilities, your goals, your future—no one else will. People believe in people who believe. It's a competitive edge.

Never give up: Have tenacity. Sticking with it until the stinkin' end is a real hallmark of a future success. Never give up.

Embrace change: Don't get comfortable; stay on the move. Never say no. Take the challenge. While others sit, be the first to say you can help, you'll try, you will...that's how you get ahead.

Ask for help: People love to mentor, to share their expertise. If you want to do something but need advice, help, or something else, just ask. If you get a no, ask someone else.

NEVER GIVE UP! NEVER GIVE UP!

Job Title: K-9 Drug-Dog Trainer

Success

I am in the K9 training business. My specialty? Police dogs. We are dedicated to breeding and training the best dope dogs on the force. Once upon a time, I worked at PetSmart, but then I joined a search and rescue training ranch that offered scent tracking and cadaver recovery. That's right, we also use dogs to search for missing bodies! The average cost of a fully trained drug dog: $5,000 to $8,000, depending on location.

Cool Stuff

This job can take you a lot of different places. Dog breeders sometimes travel the world showcasing their dogs' pedigrees. The ultimate prize…Best in Show! Dog training has different categories as well, including behavior (think Cesar Millan, the dog whisperer), scent and tracking, herding, and agility, to name a few. Did you know there's even a dog sport called "dock diving"?

Skills

Being good with animals is a no-brainer, but having great people skills is important too. The challenge is training people to control THEIR dogs. Discovering the unique communication between owner and pet is where this job comes alive. Knowledge of animal health and safety is important, while business skills and a love of physical activity are always helpful.

Education

Being a dog trainer doesn't require anything more than a high school diploma, but experience and expertise are paramount. It's not what I had planned to be, in fact, it never occurred to me until a week before I became a dog trainer. A few years later, I have my own business. I started as a breeder and kennel owner and then branched into police work. Now my police dogs are working hard in forces across the state. Local law enforcement has even hired me to train their dogs!

Financial Factor

According to the Bureau of Labor Statistics, animal trainers (dog breeders included) make an average of $35,000/year. Many make less, some make more. It depends on where you live and the extra services you provide, like grooming and kennel boarding. It's a bit of a dog-eat-dog world out there, so make sure you get your fair share by being business savvy.

If I Could Go Back

I would have taken business classes. Most of my experience was from the ground up. I hate being taken advantage of, and lacking business skills really came back to bite me.

The Truth Helps

Life is hard. "No kidding?" you say. One of the most frustrating things is that people seem to assume you know how to do something just because they do. When someone else has performed a particular task, learned a skill, or overcome a hurdle, they often forget that once all this was new to them. They probably learned by trial and error, copying someone else (whether they were right or wrong!), guessing, or just suffering through the School of Hard Knocks.

As you probably already know, if you ask for help or advice, you may:

a. get it
b. get laughed at
c. get poor advice
d. receive outdated instruction
e. hear much more than you want to

"Find out about financial aid," your parents order. "You're in charge of lining up a bus for the trip," the teacher says. "My wife is ill, I've got to leave," your boss shouts, "so get these packages shipped express today—bye!" How? Where? Who? HELP! Is there any more miserable feeling in the world than to be responsible for something and not have any idea how to accomplish it? This miserable feeling starts young. "Whadaya mean you don't know how to tie your shoes?" "Of course you know the way to the principal's office." "Haven't you learned how to do an e-mail sales campaign?" Fun, hey?

Trust me: Not only have all adults been in the same uncomfortable, clueless boat, but many still are. You don't have to settle for this, nor can you afford to. Life is full of new experiences and responsibilities. You either cope or cop out. This book is about coping. There is a secret to getting along better in this world. It's my gift to you. Any adult will confess that they wish someone had shared the current inside scoop on the real world with them when they were your age.

Do you really need to know these insider secret things? Well, I've had kids from age sixteen to recent college grads work for me in the past thirty years. Age, grades, personality, or who your dad is have absolutely nothing to do with being wise in the ways of the world. This is not something you can learn from your parents, or at school. It's as elusive as can be. Some people never discover the information you'll read in this book.

Personally, I think that up to this point, school, parents, and businesses have done a great disservice to most kids. Everything is so competitive these days. You want to get an education and you want to get a job. You want and deserve a great career where you can make a good living and make a responsible contribution as a citizen.

Most of the "stuff" you'll read in this book is not really secret at all, it's just not much talked about to so-called "kids" and that's not fair.

Read and believe.
Read and reap.
The truth helps.

Job Title: Computer Technician

Success

When you're pulling your hair out and considering throwing your computer through the window, come see me. Diagnosing a problem and fixing it is what I do best. It's not the glamorous life of fame and champagne fountains, but it's honest work in high demand. Whether it is the newest touch-screen technology or the most powerful computer graphics card, I'm constantly learning new systems and playing with the latest technology. I get major discounts too!

Job Satisfaction

The technology is the best. Part of my job is installing new hardware and software. Ripping out defective parts and replacing them is somehow extremely satisfying. When a job is finished, it's rewarding to hear a customer sigh, "How could I live without my computer?"

Skills

This isn't programming ones and zeros, but you do need a general knowledge of how a computer works—both hardware AND software. Overall, a computer technician's greatest duty is facing overwhelming challenges without blowing a fuse. Staying calm and logical is the key to solving problems quickly, while strong customer service skills will guarantee clients come back the next time the Trojans attack.

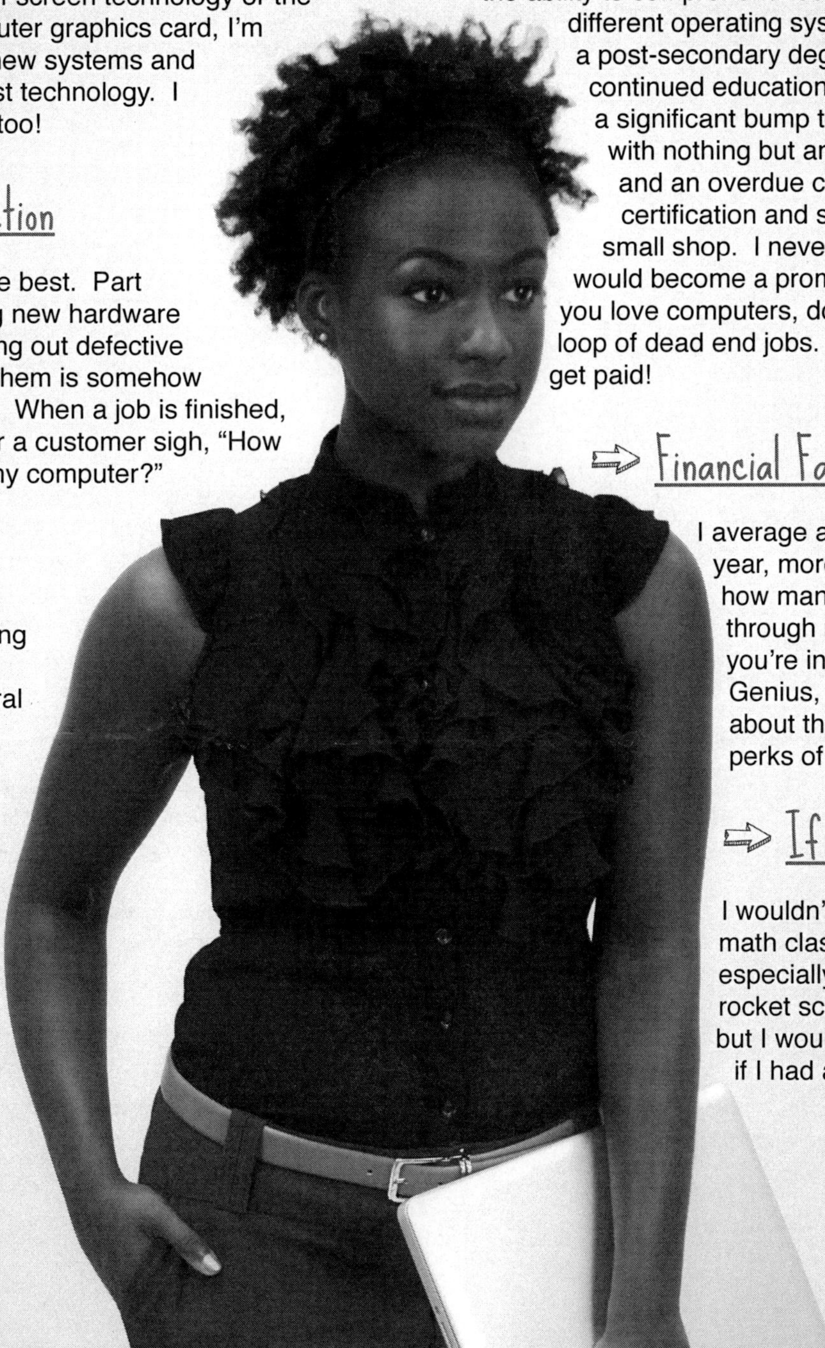

Education

Some workers enter this field with a high school diploma. However, you will need technical training, plus the ability to comprehend technical manuals and use different operating systems. Most workers have a post-secondary degree or certification, and continued education and specialization will give a significant bump to your salary. I started off with nothing but an addiction to PC games and an overdue car payment. I got my repair certification and started as an assistant in a small shop. I never thought a quick cash fix would become a promising full-time career. If you love computers, don't get stuck in an infinite loop of dead end jobs. Get educated, get training, get paid!

Financial Factor

I average around $35,000–$40,000/year, more or less depending upon how many in-home visits I schedule through my personal network. If you're interested in being an Apple Genius, I'll tell you that they make about the same amount, with all the perks of being an Apple employee.

If I Could Go Back

I wouldn't have slept through my math classes, geometry and algebra especially. Computer repair isn't rocket science (or worse, calculus), but I would have learned a lot faster if I had analytical math skills.

Daydreaming for Dollars? Nice Work if You Can Get It!

Most of the things I talk about in this book relate to work or school, which is where we spend most of our life. No matter what your situation, life can be better—but only you can make it that way.

No matter what anyone else says or thinks, I believe you probably have a LOT of great ideas. I'll bet you think about lots of different things all the time. Most of us walk around, sit at our desk, or slip off to sleep thinking about things…stuff…important stuff…little things. These thoughts are the essence of your future. Only you can know what your dreams and desires are, what your personal preferences are, and what your inclinations and intentions are. Your mind is your friend; listen to it.

If your body is made up of 98% water, your life is made up of 2% inspiration and 98% hard work. Think about it: That oral report you gave took two minutes but you probably worried about it for a week! The big game? You probably went over that winning play in your mind for a month—the same play it took only seconds to execute. The older you get, the more serious much of your "think time" becomes: *What college? Drugs? Sex? Why didn't I get that job? How am I going to get the money? Will I ever be successful?*

Daydreaming, again, hey? Good! Frankly, that's how I make my living—not writing, as much as staring at the wall for hours on end—*thinking*: about you, about my goals and how best to achieve them, about which word to use. These thoughts, like your thoughts, are important—very important. Nothing will ever come of them unless these thoughts are "captured," saved, sorted, selected, and eventually used or discarded. These are all your choices, no one else's.

Most people have no system to do this. Smart people do. Don't kid yourself: your best teachers, most successful business executives, or talented Hollywood stars have a system for keeping and recalling thoughts, facts, and ideas and choosing which to use or act on, and when.

So, make a system for yourself. If you're a genius, do it in your head in cubbyholes in your mind. Me? I'm not *that* smart. Besides, I like a backup system, like a "plan." While I don't have all the answers all the time, I do have the stuff answers are made of—and that's a smart head start.

Get a head start: Make a plan. You can change it. But thoughts on paper have a way of coming true!

Job Title: Counter-Terrorism Expert

Success

My job sounds like a spy job, right? Sometimes it is, but sometimes it's checking records, doing research, training others, and creating emergency plans. I love my job because it's demanding, exciting, and full of variety. I work behind a desk and in the field (not to be confused with in a field, which could happen!), I travel all over the world, and I'm a chameleon when I need to be—changing and blending in wherever I am.

SPY Gear

In addition to my techno-tools like my smartphones, laptops, and tablets, I also use all kinds of recording and surveillance equipment! I'm trained in explosives, including how to make, detect, and defuse them. I'm fluent in several foreign languages and have studied the cultures of many different countries, too.

Skills

Remaining calm, cool, and collected in all situations is a must. Self-confidence, discipline, and discretion are required, too. Not to brag, but I'm physically fit and can really take charge when it's needed. It's important to know how not to stand out in a crowd, how to communicate (that's where the different languages come in), and how to work with others, especially from different cultures.

Education

A military background is a huge plus! The minimum education for this job is a bachelor's degree. I did ROTC (Reserve Officer Training Corps) in high school and earned a college scholarship that way. During college, I majored in chemistry, and after college I entered the military as a Chemical, Biological, Radiological, and Nuclear Officer. I'm now in charge of a chemical unit at a large post here in the United States.

Financial Factor

I have great benefits and a lot of my pay isn't in money—it's in housing and food allowances, medical coverage, special pay, and tax benefits. If you take all that out, I still make great money—over $50,000 a year. In the private sector, there's potential to make double that, but I'd have to weigh the extra money against the great benefits I have in the military.

If I Could Go Back

I don't think I'd change a thing. ROTC helped me to learn self-confidence, discipline, the significance of physical fitness, and countless other skills I use today. It also funded my college education, and it led me to my incredible, globe-trotting career!

If the World Is Made of Words, You'd Better Learn the Language

Vocabulary is probably one of the words students hate the most. If school could make the learning of words even more boring, I honestly think they would. Why? I know vocabulary words may not be presented in school with the impact and entertainment of a rock video, but face it: the world, your life, and all that goes on in both is run by words. And if you think you don't care, well, just hope your future brain surgeon doesn't feel that way!

There is probably no single thing that will hold you back or help you forward more than just being able to write and speak in decent English. I'm not talking about spelling and grammar—you can always look up misspelled words in a dictionary and check your punctuation against a good grammar book. But only time and effort can produce an acceptable number of intelligent words that will come out of your mouth when you open it, or will be available in your head for writing down when this is called for. *And it will be.*

I'm not talking about hard words. I'm talking about plain, simple words that communicate. I'm talking about knowing what these words mean, when and how to use them, and being able to because you practice. This is not something you can cram for before a job interview or television appearance.

This is not a hard thing to accomplish. You learned to talk, didn't you? Now, just practice learning to speak correctly.

Don't have a lazy mouth.

Speak in complete sentences when you should.

Be sure you know the meaning of a word.
If you're smart, but sound ignorant, there is no one to suspect the difference.

Grow out of uh, huh, duh, and ya know?

Why do words matter so much? Because we are stuck with using words to communicate—and communication is what it's all about, especially in the real world of work. I get really aggravated when I have to explain to a freelancer what I mean when I ask for a "pro forma invoice." Or when a new hire has no idea what *facilitate* (for example) means. They are just words and terms; learn them.

There's one more thing about words. We take them for granted. Unfortunately, no one will ever take you aside and say, "Hey, you are really cute and bright, but you sound like a hick or a rap-singing mushmouth, and it spoils everything." You can take care of the "uh-uhs" and the "ya knows" yourself. Pick an adult whose speech you respect and ask them to critique you. They will be happy to help, and it's probably just a handful of words or phrases that you need to change.

(By the way, you can say whatever ya want with your friends —adults speak two languages too!)

**Manufacturing*
**Agriculture & Natural Resources*

Job Title: HVAC/R Green Tech

Success

It's practical energy conservation. Your heating, ventilation, air conditioning and refrigeration units are wasteful, wasteful, wasteful! Homes and businesses everywhere are feeling the heat to "go green." I help install and repair systems as well as advise companies on energy-saving technology and practices. I dropped out of high school to take care of my sick dad and got a job with a local electrical company. I couldn't graduate, so I studied hard to get my GED. I was making decent money, so I took HVAC classes. After working for a while I went back to school to get an HVAC engineering degree. Now I'm advising local companies throughout the southeast on how they can cut costs and stay cool.

Real Needs

You couldn't live in the southeast without us. It's too hot in the summer and too cold in the winter. On the job, I get to be on my feet, talk with customers, and see a job through. I'm working on REAL problems for REAL people.

Skills

Do you like putting things together and taking them apart? What about puzzles? Technicians need to be friendly and honest so customers are comfortable having them in their homes. A lot can be done with common sense, but nothing is ever spelled out in red. It might seem like an easy job, but I bet you don't know a thermal ventilator from a cooling coil.

Education

HVAC/R technicians usually get on-the-job training. Sometimes, apprenticeships are the best route to go, ending in certification. These days, heating and cooling systems are increasingly complex, needing better-trained technicians. If you can't find a veteran electrician to show you the ropes, check out a technical or community college for certification. Right out of the gate, you'll be certified and out making money.

Financial Factor

HVAC/R techs make about $42,000/year and work full time. Right now, the job market is HUGE. The powers that be say HVAC/R tech jobs should increase by 34%...that's way faster than normal. Average is 10–12%.

If I Could Go Back

I've always been a good people-person, but my math skills were just awful. If I hadn't dropped out, CADD and business math classes in high school would have been a big jump-start. Other than that, I would have thought twice about getting tattoos. Some people like it, but old ladies give me funny looks.

Using Your Brain by Using Your Brain

"Using your head" is the key to having "smarts." Your brain is tucked inside your thick skull for a reason, and is more than willing to help you, if you'll let it. Actually, that's its job and it gets bored when it doesn't get to use its best skills, don't you?

The overused expression that your brain is like a computer is very true. No one knows or accepts this more than creative people, such as writers and artists and musicians. For example, if I'm writing a children's mystery book and I get stumped about how to get some characters out of a mess, I can respond in several ways:

- Panic and decide I'm a really crappy writer
- Give up since I'm stumped and discard my work to-date
- Decide that since I don't have an instant answer, there isn't one
- Take a few minutes to think about my problem, why I'm stumped, where I went wrong, if I went wrong, what I want to happen next, what I don't want to happen next—then forget about it, and go on to something else

It seems like magic, but it isn't—that at some point over the next few hours or days, my brain flashes a Great Idea about how to get those characters out of hot water.

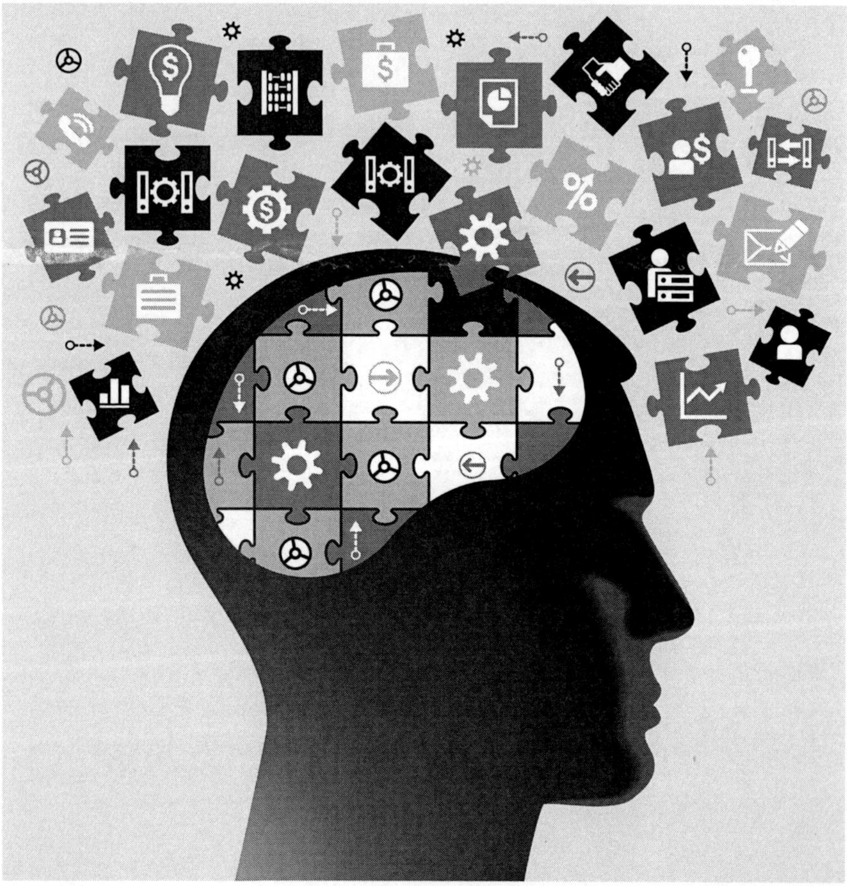

I don't know how the brain does it. When you ask, it answers by scanning its cells for stored knowledge, past experiences, or tucked-away ideas that might help. Then it converts everything you do while you're waiting for this new insight into a potential solution to the problem. The reason you often feel the answer was there all the time (once you have the answer!) is that it was—it just needed time to materialize.

What does this tell you? Well, to treat this ability—we all have it—seriously. Practice makes perfect. Setting aside some "think time" (I even put it on my calendar for big projects!)—even five minutes—lets your brain know in no uncertain terms that you need its help.

All this saves a lot of time and anxiety. Sometimes the best answer is that there is no answer needed. The other good thing is that you get to take all the credit for a Great Idea, and your brain won't mind one bit!

Job Title: Development Coordinator

Success

I'm not afraid to ask for what I want and go for it with gusto! My goal is to develop fundraising strategies and turn them into actual funds! I go wherever my job takes me—on trips, to meetings, to parties, and all kinds of other cool events—I'm always ready and excited to meet new people and cultivate connections!

Social Life

I get paid to have fun! It's true. My job requires me to talk to people, throw parties, plan big events with lots of food and entertainment, send e-mails, travel, and rub elbows with some pretty important (maybe even famous) people. Plus, since I work for a major university, I earn around $80,000 a year. Not bad, huh?

Skills

Organization and planning skills are a must! I'm outgoing and love to meet new people. I love to set and reach goals, and confidence is my strength.

Education

Funny thing, I never planned on doing this job forever. See, I was in college and needed a part time job. The development office at my university hired me. I worked as an associate for a few semesters, and one day I realized—what I was doing felt a lot more like fun than work. That's when I knew this was the career for me! I switched majors, started working in the development office full time, and earned my degree in marketing while I worked my way up to becoming the development coordinator at my alma mater! I don't have to have a degree to do my job. My experience would have been enough. Earning my degree was a personal goal of mine.

Financial Factor

It really depends on where you work...you'll make decent money no matter what, but it can vary from place to place. The range is $35,000 to $80,000, but you can make up to $95,000 or maybe even more!

If I Could Go Back

I wouldn't change anything. When I started working in the development office, I had no clue what I wanted to do for a living. I hadn't even declared a major yet! This path led me to my dream job.

Creativity: The Key to Never-ending Opportunity

There is nothing much more fun or rewarding than being creative. And, there is nothing more discouraging than to have someone not appreciate (or even make fun of) your great new idea.

This is especially frustrating because we all know that new solutions to old problems are always needed. So why are they not always welcome?

When I have younger-aged employees working for me, I expect a lot of them: good attitude, hard work, and ordinary things like being on time. What I would LOVE, but don't expect, are good ideas that contribute to a better, more efficient operation of my company.

Why don't I expect this? Because work is new to most of these employees and they concentrate on doing their job exactly as I have specified. I respect that much of their mental and physical concentration is devoted to that. Of course, it's because they're so involved with doing one (or a few) things over and over that *they* would be the most likely source of an idea to greatly improve a task.

So…maybe I really do expect some of these employees to bring me a good, practical, creative idea now and then. Do you think you have a good idea? Is that good enough?

For an idea to be beneficial to anyone, it has to be communicated, and clearly. If you rush up and tell me your idea when I'm headed out the door to a meeting, you can be sure your idea will not get much interest or attention from me. If you charge up to me and tell your idea non-stop-without-a-breath, I may get an inkling that you're onto something—but what? And if your great idea is impossible, requires a humongous bank loan or the Incredible Hulk, I might not be too receptive.

But what if you ask if you can see me the next day for five minutes to hear an idea you have that will save time and money? I'm no dummy! "Sure!" The next day you ask me to come to your workstation, where you demonstrate exactly what you are talking about. "You're right!"

The world loves a person with a better idea. I now love you. You feel good about yourself. You'll feel better when I surprise you with a bonus check made available from the savings you've uncovered, and offer you a promotion to an area that needs some more initiative and practical real world solutions.

FYI: This is how the real world works.

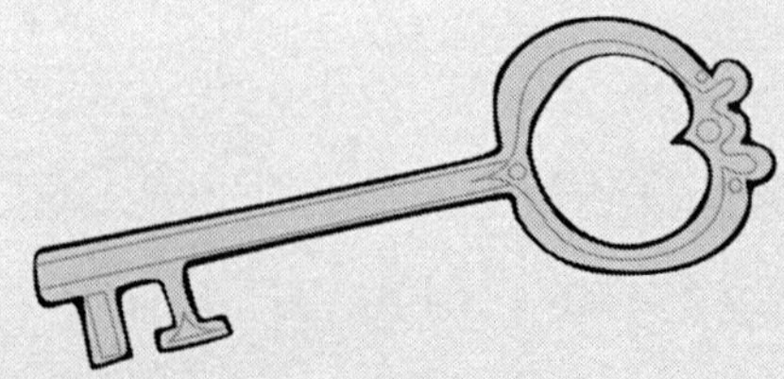

Job Title: CADD Architectural Drafter

Success

There are boatloads of drafting careers, but I stayed traditional. Architectural drafters do the technical floor plans for homes, executive offices, and community buildings. The word jock describes the high-school me, with a near-perfect free throw record—big fish, small pond, I guess. When I didn't get any athletic scholarship offers, I was pretty angry, but my friend was joining the military, so I tagged along. Math came easy, but I didn't want to be a mathematician—*bleh*. My military training in computer aided drafting and design gave me something useful to do. Yeah, Monday after a long weekend can be tedious, but seeing a finished product based on my design—that's a good feeling.

Education

I didn't just walk in off the street and get a drafting job. Drafters do technical designs for everything from microchips to skyscrapers and such. Get a jump on the competition in your high school math, computer technology, design, and, where available, drafting courses. Starting off in drafting means getting an Associate degree. Get it at a technical or community college—proof that you have advanced drafting skills and know how to handle a CADD machine. I easily swapped my military training for civilian work. It's true I had to go back to school for architecture, but the military helped me get it done.

New Tricks

The newest CADD technology can do 3D printing, which means some day construction might be completely automated! Put in the floor plan, press a button, and *BAM!* out comes a house! Maybe not anytime soon, but fun to think about.

Financial Factor

Most drafters make around $47,000/year, and job security really pays off. A good drafter is a keeper. Unless you're a bad employee, you can expect to find work and keep work.

Skills

I really get satisfaction from pointing out an architect's design flaws—that's where critical thinking pays off. I have trouble focusing, and active listening didn't come easy, but it's really important. Other things you need to survive: communication and teamwork, technical skills (CADD), and time management. ATTENTION to detail, too—kiss your job goodbye if a wall gets built two feet in the wrong direction.

If I Could Go Back

Looking back, sports taught me a lot about being a hard worker and a team player. It's every kid's dream to be the next big game-changer, but it doesn't have to be in sports. I don't regret my athletic days, but I'm glad they weren't the glory days. The best are yet to come.

Image

Nothing is probably more important to each of us than our image, our identity—how we want others to see us. Companies spend millions of dollars each year presenting their identity to the public. McDonald's wants your parents to see them as a wholesome company, concerned with good nutrition. They want kids to perceive them as yummy and fun. Of course, they want their stockholders to think of them as smart cookies, talented at making money.

You're no different. You have many audiences for your image. A person with "smarts" understands that and uses it to his or her advantage. If you want your friends to think of you as that wild and crazy kid with the green hair, that's great. But you'll go a lot further in this world if you modify your image for your teacher in the classroom, your parents when they want to take you out to eat, or your potential boss when you're interviewing for a job.

What's wrong? Does it seem like a compromise to be one way to one person and put on a different appearance for another? Don't sell yourself so short. We all have many-faceted personalities and there's nothing wrong with showing your best side when it's appropriate or to your benefit. If your mom wore her flip-flops and jeans to the bank to ask for a loan, you'd think she was crazy. Dressing nice for a job interview is no more compromise than running home afterwards and putting on your purple mini-skirt in time for the party.

The most important word in image is—sincerity. Be yourself. Your very best self may be quite formal or still pretty casual. The adjustments in your image for a particular situation should be motivated by respect—for yourself and others. Is it OK with you if your dad comes to graduation in his sloppy-Saturday-around-the-house-watching-the-ballgame clothes? Or do you hope, in all sincerity, that his image as the father of a graduating senior is more respectful than that?

Image is more than clothes. It's attitude, language, authenticity, and being genuine. Adults, especially job interviewers, can always spot the real thing.

Be the real thing.

It's our choices... that show what we truly are, far more than our abilities.

—J.K. Rowling

Manufacturing
Transportation, Distribution & Logistics

Job Title: Motorsport Tech

Success

Have you ever changed a tire? I could do it for you in less than 6 seconds. As an auto mechanic I've worked my way up into the world of professional racing. My team works on F1 racers, testing performance and efficiency to make sure our car is the optimal racing machine. On the track, we work under pressure, anticipating problems and making repairs with perfect accuracy. It's not an easy job, but I make a good living, and the work environment, well, it's where I like to be.

Cool Tools

Did you know that I use all sorts of power tools, wrenches, jacks, and hydraulic lifts to get the job done. In the old days, a good mechanic used only basic tools and his/her senses to diagnose a problem, but computers have changed everything. Now I play with some of the most high-tech smart chips and onboard computers.

Skills

I'll tell you, good eyes, ears, nose, and an attention to detail are the nuts and bolts that hold this job together. If you like working with your hands, taking things apart and putting them back together, this job is right for you. The first thing I do is diagnosis; I check the electrical system, the computerized electronics, or perhaps the fuel and refrigeration system.

Ladies, this isn't just a job for men. My wife is the best electrical mechanic I know.

Education

I'm basically a car doctor, but I didn't get a Ph.D. I thought education was for somebody else, but after high school, I got sick of retail customers real fast, so I got my GED while working as an automotive assistant. I learned quick that the days of the uneducated grease monkey are over. Upcoming auto mechanics have got to have vocational skills and adapt to new technology. I enrolled at a community college and got my applied science degree, and later got my automotive technology certificate. On-the-job training taught me about fuel systems, and that's how I got into racing. It took a while to work my way up to Formula One, but that's a lot of greasy history.

Financial Factor

A shop automotive mechanic working at a car dealer or private repair shop can expect to make around $35,000/year. Combining business savvy with automotive prowess could lead you to opening your own shop and risk it all! If you've got other talents, you might make an extra buck teaching automotive repair or doing private custom design.

If I Could Go Back

I would have been a dentist. That's a joke, but really, it's hard to look back when you're in the fast lane.

Attitude

Attitude. Don't you hate it when someone suggests that yours stinks?

Attitude is probably the most important part of your identity. It speaks most sincerely about how you really are. It cannot be disguised with green hair or hide behind a business card.

A good attitude can overcome the most humble of surroundings—whether background, economic status, home, car, or clothing. A poor attitude can make even the brightest, most attractive person undesirable.

Everyone has an attitude. Most manifestations of our attitude are habit. We pretty much know when our attitude stinks and when it doesn't. Having the maturity to question the less appealing aspects of our attitude and focusing to improve those areas is a good idea.

One thing to remember about attitude is "Point of view is everything." You and your parents may have very different attitudes about your taking their new car to another town. You probably really do understand their concerns, and they probably don't blame you for what you want to do. But do you see their point of view enough to counter it, not with arguments, but with the kind of language that communicates understanding of their concerns enough for them to believe you have the "right" attitude about the seriousness and importance of their point of view? If so, your "good" attitude may net you a positive answer, or at least an acceptable compromise.

One attitudinal flaw that knows no age limits is the person who always says, *"I assumed." "I assumed you meant I was supposed to work next Saturday." "I assumed you wouldn't care if I borrowed twenty bucks from your wallet." "I assumed I was going to pass the course."* The lesson is: ask questions; don't assume.

Attitude is a smile and your style. It's courtesy and creativity. You can be shy and still share. You can be cute or crazy. "He's got a great attitude" is not a judgment on *how* you are; it's another's opinion of *who* you are.

And speaking of judgments, interviewers make quick ones.

Your attitude, not your aptitude, will determine your altitude

— Zig Ziglar

Job Title: Psychological Profiler

Success

Why do people commit serious crimes? I'm not talking about convenience store muggers or drug addicts. I investigate the darker side of the human mind. I build profiles to better understand abnormal behavior and the criminal motivation. A lot of my work is documentation and analysis, but I'm a criminal investigation/psychology hybrid and actively involved in crime scene analysis. Warning: To be good at this job you might start thinking like a criminal. The saying goes: it takes one to know one!

Cool Stuff

Most psychological profilers work for the FBI and hold special agent status! I analyze handwriting, record evidence, and use documented criminal behavior patterns to aid an ongoing investigation. Other employers are the CIA and private investigators on hot or cold cases. Now more and more criminal profilers are being hired for full-time police investigations.

Skills

Patience, confidence, and a strong stomach are good qualities. You'll need beefy critical thinking and analytical skills as well as the ability to read data and scientific documents. The mind can be a scary place, so a strong interest in human behavior will help keep you sane.

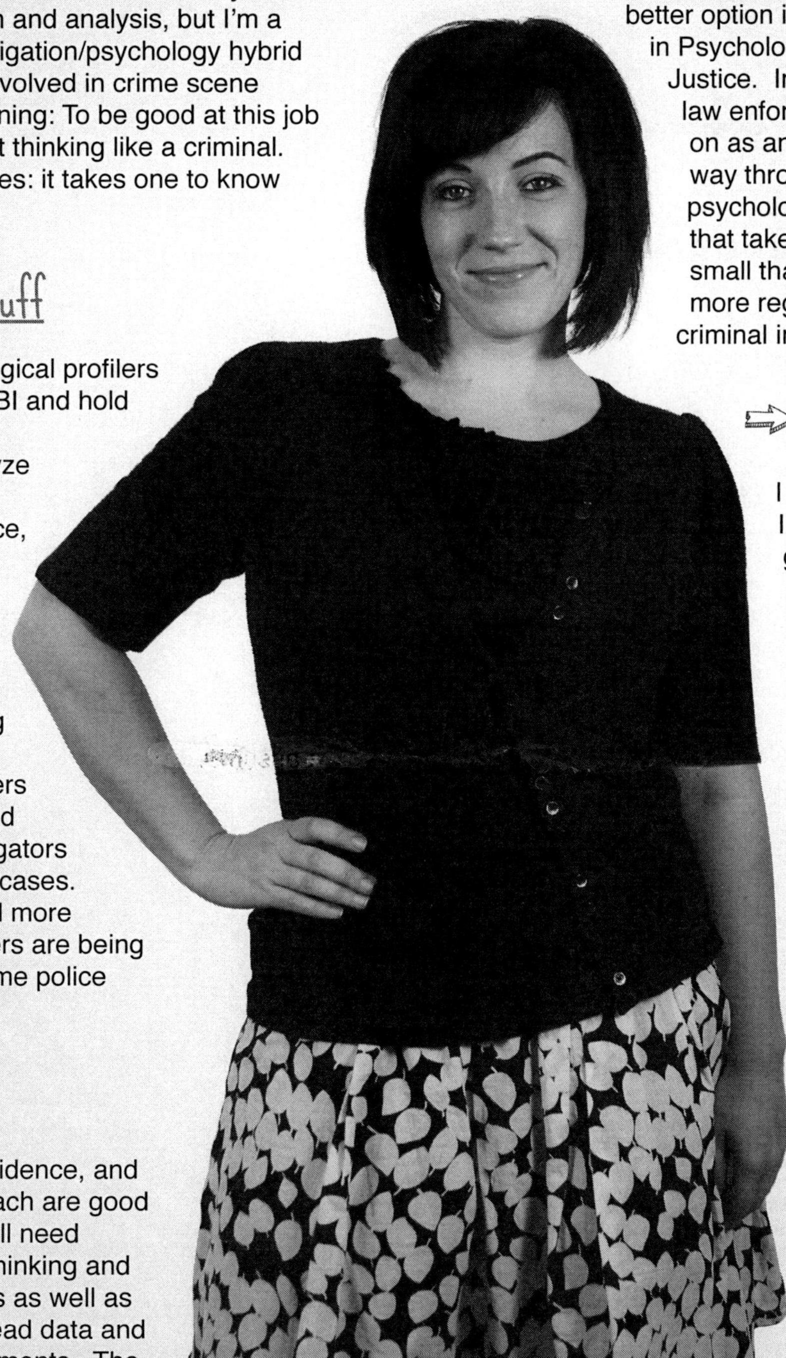

Education

Degrees are a must! I double majored in psychology and criminal justice—talk about late night studying! The better option is to first earn a Bachelor's degree in Psychology and then a Master's in Criminal Justice. Investigation experience with local law enforcement goes a long way. I signed on as an assistant investigator to pay my way through a Master's degree in forensic psychology. Be forewarned: it's a tough road that takes real mental grit. The field is so small that many psychological profilers work more regularly in crime-scene analysis and criminal investigation.

Financial Factor

I make around $65,000/year, but I'm young and my salary will only go up. Regular psychologists and psychiatrists average $85,000/year. Salaries will vary depending on where you live, your employer, and how many cases you have. Unfortunately, the big money is in high crime-rate places like D.C. or working for the FBI. Remember, the competition in this business is cutthroat.

If I Could Go Back

I would have taken high school more seriously. College is not cheap, and a scholarship would have saved my parents and me a lot of money! Don't get me wrong, I did okay in high school, good enough to get into a small college, not a major university, but I could've saved myself some killer loan money.

Resource Sorcery

One of the primary errors made when applying for a job is not finding out about the company in advance. You might think that asking, "What do you do here?" in your interview is thoughtful, considerate, and logical. *Wrong*. Especially when the question is preceded by the equally logical statement, "I'm sure I can do a good job for you." *How do you know if you don't know what we do?* the interviewer wonders.

Resources for the future can be anything:

family connections **excellent grades** **job experience**

But, **preparation** **good listening skills**

and **attention to details**

are also good resources.

Adults make great resources. It's difficult to turn down a person who asks for help, especially when it's clear that they are already trying to help themselves.

You're lucky today to have the web, but get more creative than that. Visit a company in advance. Call for a package of information or pick one up. Become a customer of that company, if that is appropriate and possible.

Resources=results

Effectively using resources is often a big part of any job. Prove that you are very resourceful and detail-driven by being prepared. Don't tell what you *can* do, show what you *have* done.

Job Title: DaVinci Surgical System Operator

Success

Some surgeons really like cutting people open. Not me. I'd rather be on the cutting edge of technology. The da Vinci Surgical System is a human-operated robot that allows me to perform delicate operations through the smallest incision possible. It gives me a 3D stereoscopic view of your insides, and the system seamlessly translates all my hand, finger and wrist movements into real-time movement of surgical instruments. Steady now, this machine requires special training. One wrong movement and you'll hear the thing surgeons HATE to say...Oops!

Cool Stuff

Remote surgery—when this technology becomes more common, a surgeon in Canada could operate on a patient far away in India. Also, the precision is great for operations on cancerous tumors and delicate heart operations.

Skills

Can you handle life or death situations? Don't sweat the small stuff, right? But a few things you'll need: great dexterity and hand-eye coordination, sharp attention to detail, and strong decision-making skills. Confidence helps. Have you ever heard a doctor say, "You are going to live! Maybe..." Most of all, you need to have patience...and patients.

Education

Do you like school? I hope so. Surgeons go through about 12 years or more of college and residency! First, you need a four-year undergraduate degree, then four years of medical school, and finally a period of residency in a hospital (usually five years). To be a da Vinci operating surgeon, you also need special machine training. Warning: there is a steep learning curve. Being a surgeon isn't for everyone, and doing robotic surgery requires the highest skill level. I started off in a small Tifton high school, and now I'm one of the first surgeons in Savannah qualified to operate the da Vinci system!

Financial Factor

You might be in school until you're 30 years old, but surgeons make an average of $166,000/year or more! With great responsibility comes great reward.

If I Could Go Back

I would have taken every "ology" course in high school. In college, I was really digging Shakespeare's love sonnets—so I wasted some time in unnecessary classes. I wonder... whatever happened to the cute girl sitting next to me?

Hanging…or Hang Gliding?

Can't do anything right? Think that's a feeling you grow out of? Don't hold your breath.

Getting along with others, achieving your goals, getting what you want out of life, being the great person you know you are takes a lot of effort. What's discouraging is when you work hard, but things still don't go your way.

It's tempting to give up. Why bother? But hanging in there is just part of the job.

Often, things that go wrong are not even your fault. You may clash with others, believe life isn't fair, think nothing's ever going to work out. Don't quit. Time, exhaustion, confusion, lack of money, and other frustrations may prevent you from taking a straight path to success. (Note: There is NO straight path to success.) Failure, struggle, missteps, backsteps, and sidesteps all eventually lead to what you want if you just hang in there.

One advantage of this seemingly unfortunate circuitous path to your goal is that you often learn that what you thought you wanted turned out not to be true at all. Often, it's the opportunity that comes after you fail that leads you to what's really the cool career for you.

This is the real world. Have a little faith, a lot of trust. Go for it and keep going for it. Just keep struggling along in the general direction you want to go—you'll get there.

In the meantime, stay out of trouble. (You can overcome trouble, too, but it sure is a lot of trouble.) Avoid self-defeating patterns. Have some tact. Be diplomatic. You'll be surprised at what can happen when you hang in there and keep plugging away.

One day it will feel like it all worked out for the best…even if it doesn't work out like you expected, meaning **EVEN BETTER!**

Job Title: Crime-Scene Cleanup

Success

This job is certainly "no guts, no glory." To put it simply, the medical examiner takes the body, and crime-scene cleaners take everything else. As a private biohazard recovery company co-owner, I make over $100,000/year. Our main tasks are cleaning blood off walls and small family trinkets, disposing of furniture, ripping up stained carpet, dealing with decomposed bodies or the loose remains of victims. Sometimes I'm called in to clear out rusty needles and chemicals from police-raided drug labs. No worry about germs—all work is done wearing a hot, heavy Hazmat suit. It's all worth the effort when we spare the survivors the hurt and pain of cleaning up a traumatic mess.

Danger Factor

My environment is a minefield of bodily fluids, airborne diseases, and flammable chemicals. After 9/11, biohazard recovery companies in New York had a full time job responding to anthrax contamination threats. It's a dangerous, dirty job. Our motto: Stay safe, don't lose your head.

Skills

You need a strong stomach and a willingness to do thankless work. Knowledge of public health and safety are essential. It's not all gristle and gore. People skills are sometimes required for talking with survivors.

Education

No college degree required. Actually, many entry-level employees only have a high-school diploma, but experience is gold, and technical training is nice to have. Many people who pursue this field had previous jobs in Public Health and Safety or worked in hospitals handling biohazard materials. Before opening my business, I was a paramedic, so it helps to have "seen it all."

Financial Factor

Don't tell your mother, but crime pays. An entry-level cleaner can expect around $35,000/year. After a few years in a big market, that salary can grow to $70,000–80,000/year. There's potential to make a six-figure killing if you open your own business. Who thought a cleaning business would make me $100,000/year? As always, high crime areas like big cities mean more business.

If I Could Go Back

My experience as a paramedic is invaluable—almost as helpful as the years I spent addicted to *CSI*. I quickly learned that working for an employer wasn't for me. If I could go back, I'd have checked out local business classes before starting my own. In the end though, I made my career on gut instinct.

Responsibility

Responsibility. You swear you want it. And yet, the first time you're expected to make a decision—you panic, or avoid it, or pass the buck.

Making a decision is one of the hardest skills to learn. Practice still won't make perfect. But you'll never have responsibility until you're willing to stick your neck out and make a decision, then stick by it, or change it if that becomes smart.

How to make a decision:

Is there a decision to be made? If so, exactly what is it you must decide? Do you need more information before you can make a decision? Must the decision be made now, or is later OK?

Once you can answer these questions, you have a real head start in making a decision. Complicated decisions may require discussions with other people. Write down the pluses and minuses. Who will it affect? What are the consequences? Will the decision be irrevocable?

When your thoughts are on paper, it may be clear what you should do. You may not like the decision you have to make. It may be the wrong decision, one you'll have to correct later, if possible. But everyone respects the decision maker. Everyone knows decision making is a tough task.

The nice thing about making decisions is that it becomes easier with experience. You realize that while drastic decisions can mean drastic results, most decisions can be adjusted later. After all, there are only two choices: making the best decision you can with the information you have, or not making the decision and leaving your life to fate. That is *your* decision.

I love employees who can make a decision on their own. I often don't care if they are right or wrong as much as I care that they can tell me why they decided to do or not do something. They have done more than make a decision. They have taken responsibility—something I often can't give away! And that's a decision I respect—*and reward.*

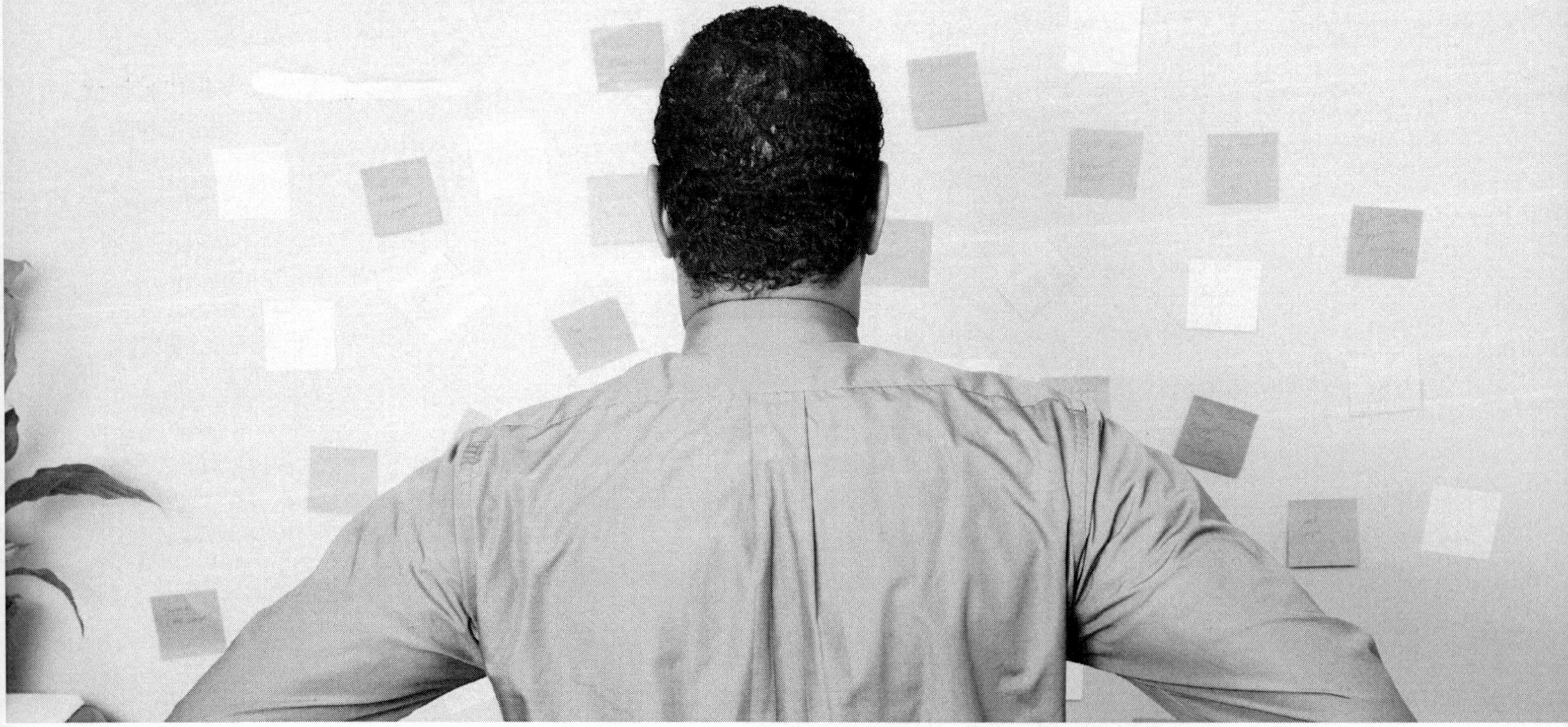

Job Title: Motion Graphics Designer

Success

Get paid for your creativity? I started when I was eleven, kind of. I had a makeshift business drawing and selling $2 stories to my friends at school. I don't think I actually turned a profit, but I didn't care back then. My job now handles a little bit of everything in the design process, like making sure the visual graphics in a film, animation, or commercial are surprising, well-crafted, and entertaining. The career is flexible—lots of different ways to work—so I figured why not expand my portfolio? Right now, I'm qualified to design for video production and internet advertising, but I really want to do what some of my friends are doing—TV special effects, or maybe mobile gaming.

Technological Art

Technology doesn't make art, humans do, but the industry runs on improved technology. New touch-screens have made my computer canvas virtually touchable, moldable, and dynamic. Motion graphics designers need to have experience in video production and computer graphic design. We use a lot of technology, it's true, but I still think I'm an artist at heart. I still like to close my MacBook, put pencil to paper, and let the creativity flow.

Skills

You need a passion to create—some people have it, many don't. To get you moving, you'll need an artistic sense of depth, space, and geometry. Computer, software, and technical skills can all be learned, but if you can't navigate basic computer programs, my job would drive you insane.

Education

I consider myself a visual person, like for some reason when I sit alone, I catch myself finding all the angles in a room and visualizing lines that might intersect (I really do). But even if you're a natural, getting training and an education is key. To be employed, you'll need a Bachelor's degree, with coursework like CADD, interactive media, and web design. Start building your portfolio early—a good showing can get you into prime-time employment. In my experience, school counts, but the measure of a good artist is seen in the work, not in the diploma.

Financial Factor

The phrase "starving artists" is outdated. Average salary for a motion graphics designer is $50,000, but it really depends on how resourceful and creative you are. Don't be afraid to show your skills and ask for what you're worth.

If I Could Go Back

I would go way back in time and visit Van Gogh, ask him why he cut his ear off. His *Starry Night* inspired my first successful portfolio piece—so I'd like to say thanks.

Time is Valuable

Time is the most valuable resource you have. Therefore, time management is an essential skill. Time can be your enemy or friend. Good habits you set now will be an asset in all your future endeavors.

You don't have time for everything; choose wisely. Good time management is logical. I'm impressed with the employees who always have time to prioritize their day, and leave their workstation clean at the end of the day.

"Five Hundred Twenty-Five Thousand Six Hundred Minutes, Five Hundred Twenty-Five Thousand Moments so Dear..." *(from Rent)*

Think about it!

Job Title: Climatologist: World Watcher

Success

I feel successful, but I know the job is bigger and broader than just me. Growing up in Kansas, I've always felt exposed to the weather, storms sometimes just coming out of nowhere. After specializing in hydrology, I moved to Florida to monitor the southeastern drought. I'm a climatologist, but I take it more seriously than a title. I'm more like a world watcher because everything is affected by our climate and everything we do (or don't do) affects our world. I like seeing the big picture so I work with other climatologists, meteorologists, environmental firms, etc., to create a worldwide information network of up-to-date climate maps. Maybe then we'll see where this world is going, what weather is blowing our way.

Whether the Weather

Weather predictors used to be superstitious, but now our chances aren't entirely thrown to the winds. Satellite imaging and complex computation models changed the game. Tracking average rainfall, highs and lows, and cloud cover is one area, but climatologists consult with private companies, state and federal governments, or build reports to change energy laws. I sure would like to sit down with Congress just to talk about the weather—this isn't small talk anymore.

Skills

Math and science are the bread and butter. I would suggest being computer-friendly, because today's climatologists use the most advanced supercomputing technology. An interest in weather isn't a bad start either, or maybe conservation motives like mine.

Education

Not to rain on your parade, but you need a Bachelor's degree in Climatology, Meteorology, or Atmospheric Science. I remember taking classes like physics, statistics, computer science, oceanography, and on and on. Oh...and thermodynamics. I stayed in school to avoid the real world, and went on to get my Master's degree, and will probably go back for my Ph.D, but right now I'm mostly content, at least with my job.

Financial Factor

The average salary range is $55,000-$100,000/year. Usually, the higher your education, the higher your salary, but don't let that get you down. Go for what you're passionate about; otherwise, you'll never make a difference.

If I Could Go Back

I guess I would have explored more before specializing. I went into the research field, building better data collection and models, but I didn't stop to look around and see what opportunities there were. Looking at the big picture is difficult when you're so small.

Plan

The one thing about not having a plan is that failure will come as a complete surprise!

There's either plan, or muddle through life. See if I care. See if anyone cares. But if you wonder how your friends got that job, that scholarship, well, they didn't just stumble blindly on them. A plan can be as simple as just really wanting something badly and working hard for it.

I seldom see young employees who actually plan on getting a promotion or a raise. Did they think it would just be luck? Or how cute they were? Or how polite? "Wait and see" is *not* a plan.

You make a plan so you can change it. Having a plan can change your life. If you read autobiographies of successful people, you'll learn that they *planned* for success. Not in some general way, but as specifically as possible. Not much went according to their plan, of course (hey, this is real life!), but at least they knew what they were deviating from and when to get back on track or go with the new flow. Either way, they eventually got to their destination.

Set priorities for your day, week, month, quarter, semester, school year, summer, and beyond. As part of your plan, have immediate, short term, mid-term, and long- term goals.

Planning is smart. Getting a good job may be a short- or long-term goal. But if your plan includes learning about the job, building skills for the job, interning at such a job, getting a required certificate for the job, then what could be a tortuous, long-term process may prove to be much quicker and easier than you ever believed.

Job Title: Market Research Analyst

Success

Would you like to know how you'll die? Maybe not, but if you want to know what the next BIG thing is before it explodes, this is your field. Before launching a new product or service, companies rely on me to collect and examine data about consumers' wants, needs, and buying habits. Best thing about my job: I can have a huge variety of responsibilities! In a single day, I might taste test a new flavor of Skittles, work the numbers on a "brand" new branding campaign for a fashion line, or analyze political polls. People think it's all smoke and mirrors, but there's not much guesswork. It's just people, statistics, and the future of our business markets. The occasional gamble pays off—a well informed gamble, that is.

The Life

I get to test products before they hit the market. New iPad? I'll try that, thank you. A big part of my job is talking to people. I get to run my mouth, ask opinions, and pose questions too touchy for a "respectable" party.

Skills

Take it from me, confidence will take you to high places with important people. Math skills, critical thinking, and communication are ALL do or die, and I handle lots of data, prepare reports, and make presentations, so interpretation and analysis are essential. Hmmm, what else? Time management, coordination, persuasion, and speaking and writing all need to be fine-tuned. Can you handle that?

Education

Minimum requirement is a Bachelor's degree in Market Research or something like that. I went to college on a cello scholarship, but figured a business degree would help me pay back loans quicker. I took a heavy course-load in mathematics and computer science as well. Really, I was that shy kid with glasses in college, and I always bombed my interviews. It took getting my Master's degree to make me finally grow up—speech and business communication classes were the devil. No pain, no gain, right? Now I'm working for a regional marketing firm.

Financial Factor

Average salary is $60,000/year. On top of a nice paycheck, this job field is expected to increase by 41%!!! EVERY industry employs market research analysts, which means finding a job won't be like pulling teeth.

If I Could Go Back

Some days when my life is a mess, my boss is rushing me on deadlines, and the CEO of Coke won't call me back, I consider picking up the cello again. And I do at home in my spare time. It calms my nerves.

Money

If there's one thing adults probably wished they'd learned at your age, it's how to manage money. Money will be a part of your life all your life.

Learn to budget, to anticipate, and to correct money errors in real time. By errors, I don't mean mathematical. I mean if you make a charge on a credit card, wash it out by paying it off by the end of the month, and don't make additional charges until you do.

Learn the real words and terms for money. I once had a friend who was young and shy. She felt her skills would not be evident to her job interviewer. She asked what I thought she should say to her potential new boss, so he'd understand that she was not a business novice.

"Say that you know what accounts receivable are," I advised. I knew any business person would be impressed with a 17-year-old who knew that accounts receivable are what other people owe you.

You have assets. You have liabilities. Money can work for you, or against you. Or, money can be like water in an open bathtub drain.

Create a one-page form that shows what you own and its value, and what you owe. Check this "balance sheet" weekly and see how you can improve your net worth.

Money management is not magic. Ten percent of your paycheck faithfully saved can avoid a lot of debt pain. Waste is a good way to never have anything. So is squandering your money; once it's spent, it's gone, so be sure you really do want or need the new __________.

Most importantly, don't fall into money traps. When I hear college grads on television whining about their $60,000 in student debt (unless they were in medical school), I laugh. My kids worked their way through college. It took a little longer and wasn't as much fun, but they were debt-free at the end.

And, as I recall, they cooked instead of eating out, drove used cars, and other money-saving measures. Your money, your choice.

By the way, it takes many years to pay off debt and the longer you take, the more you have to pay because of the interest on that debt.

It's a lot more fun to buy a new convertible with your new debt-free paycheck—*I know.*

Job Title: Dental Hygienist

Success

Tenth grade year, I had five cavities filled and two root canals. The whole experience was awful, not to mention my dentist smelled like rotten cabbage. I hated the dentist's office—the look, that little scraping tool, and the drill. Never in a million years did I think I'd end up working for a dentist, but I'll be honest with you for a moment—dental hygiene is a great career (now that I'm not a patient). I have normal working hours, great pay, and I try to be so much nicer than the doctor. I'm really family oriented, and I like to keep close tabs on my six younger brothers—they're a mess! Being a dental hygienist means I can get a job in just about any place, including a dental office close to my family.

Skills

A good, upbeat attitude is key, and I really love talking to patients—it keeps me smiling. You need nimble fingers for digging around in people's mouths and comfortable shoes because you'll be on your feet most of the day.

Education

I got my Associate degree in two years. Most hygienists go to vocational school like I did, and the state government requires certification. If you are not at least interested in science courses and the human body in high school, then two years of an Associate degree in Dental Hygiene will be like pulling teeth.

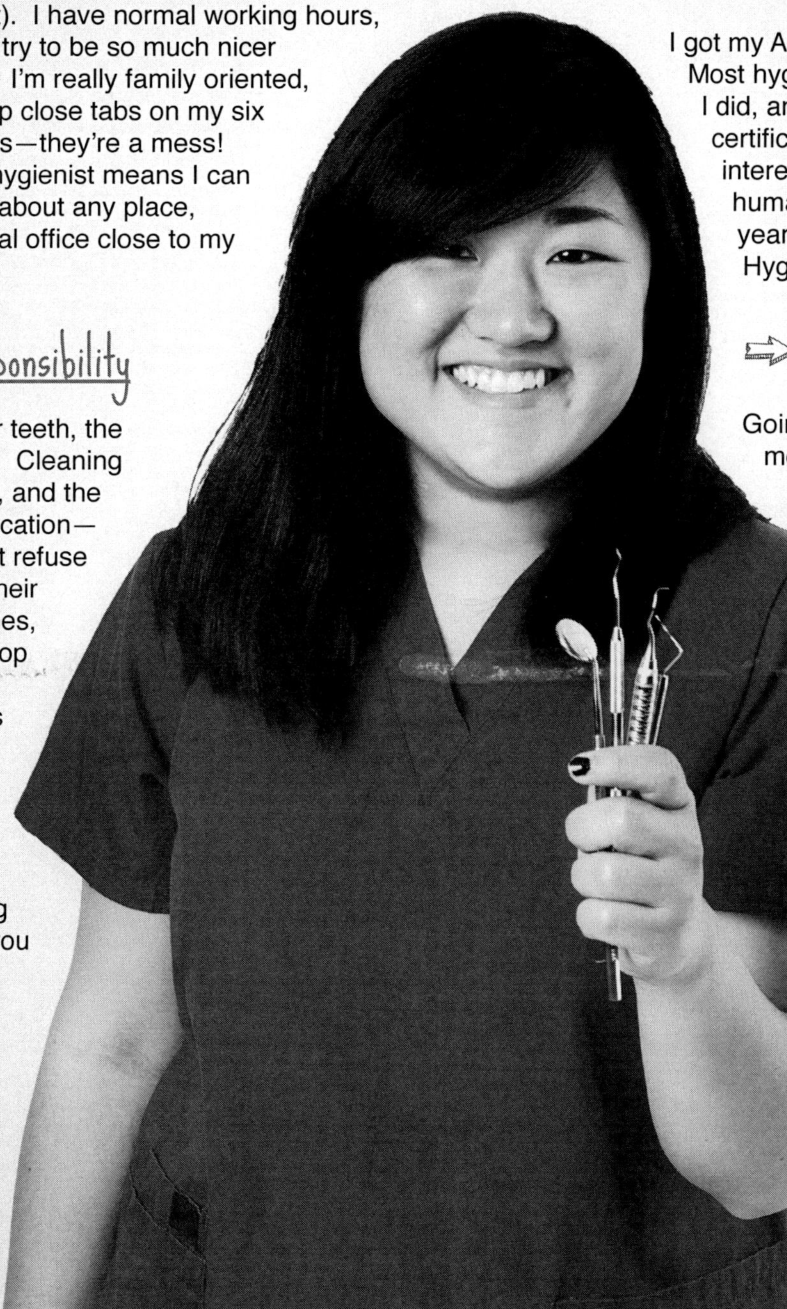

Job Responsibility

The nastier your teeth, the harder my work. Cleaning is half the battle, and the other half is education—some people flat refuse to take care of their teeth. Other times, I take and develop x-rays and keep track of patient's health records. My job as the hygienist is to help the doctor do as little tooth pulling as possible. If you fall off your bike and put holes in your smile—well, I can't help that!

Financial Factor

Going into a profession JUST for the money is a bad idea. That being said, I make around $65,000/year. There's plenty of room to make more (or less) depending on where you live. Either way, it's not a bad job, considering the dental and health coverage I get. I usually have Fridays off too, and sometimes I work for another local dentist. Life's good.

If I Could Go Back

I would have taken better care of my teeth. Three of my teeth are crowned, and even though I get great dental coverage, there's no replacement for a strong set of healthy teeth.

Calling All Nervous Wrecks

If I had to pick the number one thing I have seen new employees panic over, it would be a phone call. Learn to make a productive phone call in front of others. Believe it or not, not everything can be done by e-mail or text messaging.

Making an effective phone call is a lot like playing *Monopoly*, chess, or bridge. There's someone on the other side. You have a goal—to get or share information.

Prepare for a phone call like you would any other task. Get over the intimidation of having someone listen to your conversations. The best way is to speak up, no matter how unconfident you feel.

Job Title: Robotics Engineer

Success

A dog may be man's best friend, but for a quadriplegic man, a robot that helps him scratch an itch or shave his face is way more useful! I'm a robotics engineer. My job is to develop the latest humanoid robot technology. Inspired by the flexible people around us, we give a wide range of bending, lifting, bouncing, and twisting to an otherwise lifeless hunk of junk (modern-day Frankenstein?). But my passion is helping people. I engineered new bio-robotic technology to give veteran amputees affordable prosthetic arms. Oh, no, my job does not stop there! Humanoid robotics is everywhere, from building more efficient factory robots to engineering voice-responsive house cleaners. Star Wars robots like R2-D2 might be a long way off, but my job isn't science fiction. Robotics careers are here now, revolutionizing the future.

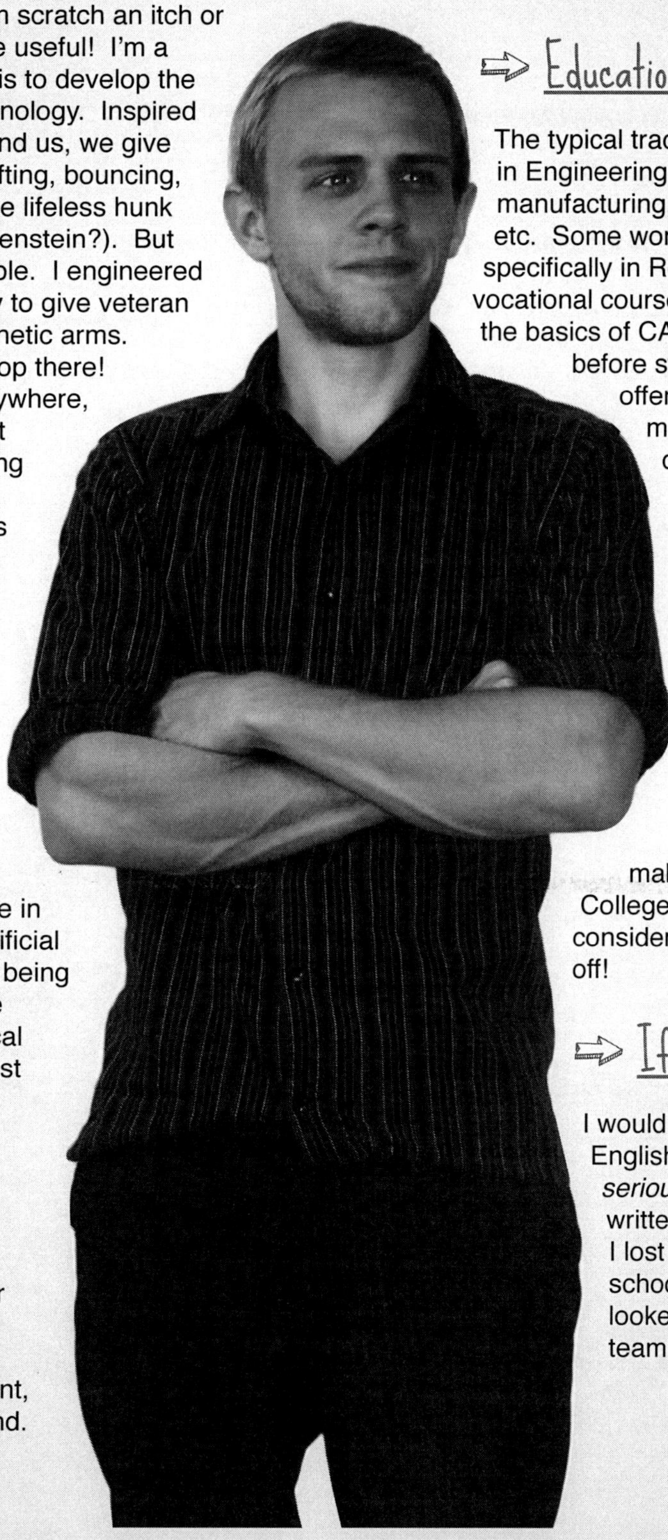

Future is Now

Did you know that robotic pets are on the market today? Cleaning robots are in people's homes. Weak artificial intelligence (AI) robots are being used in military intelligence missions, in delicate surgical procedures, and in the latest smart-home designs.

Skills

Can you handle tedious tasks? Technical computer skills are everything. Robotics is hands-on, so don't be afraid to experiment, manipulate, and play around. A love of automation is a must, and an understanding of electrical circuits and input/output technology can be learned in training. Robotics engineers need to be detail-oriented, playful, and practical.

Education

The typical track is a Bachelor's degree in Engineering, with study areas including manufacturing, electrical, mechanical, industrial, etc. Some work requires a Master's degree specifically in Robotics. I started by taking vocational courses in high school to already have the basics of CADD and robotics programming before starting college. Technical schools offer robotics training while some major universities offer full robotics departments. BEST ADVICE: Get a head start by taking high school science and math courses. If your school partners with a technical college, dual enroll and get hands-on playtime (training) before you apply to a technical school or university.

Financial Factor

The average robotics engineer makes $60,000 to $90,000/year. College loans can weigh you down, but consider programming a robot to pay them off!

If I Could Go Back

I would have taken my speech and English classes more seriously… *seriously.* Engineers need strong written and oral communication skills. I lost a robotics competition in high school because my project description looked like a child's coloring book. My team was thrilled—not!

Tools of the Trade

In our offices, we have a lot of meetings. *(Grrrrrr…I hate meetings!)* Any employee who shows up without a notepad and pencil is banished from the room. (Did they think nothing important enough to write down would be said?) Always come prepared.

Get a calendar. Keep track of your affairs. Have a place for the business stuff of your life. Have lists, notes, files. Yes, on a computer counts—if you back it up. ("The computer ate my stuff" is too much like "The dog ate my homework.")

Learn to make a flow chart. A flow chart is just the sequence of events in a task to be performed, shown on paper using boxes and arrows. It's used for planning, organizing, and decision making. There's simple software for it, or, uh, just draw some circles, squares, and arrows.

Have a calculator and know how to use it. Also know how to "do the math" without a calculator. *Seriously.*

Got a cell phone? The first thing to **learn is where the MUTE button is**; use it.

Read the daily paper. Business operates in the real world. Be part of it or be left out; and yes, the sports page counts too.

Job Title: Dietician

Success

I'm not rail thin. I'm not starving myself. And I'm certainly not letting good food go to waste. As a dietician, people expect me to look like a celebrity. Truth is, celebrities usually aren't healthy. I'm a clinical dietician, meaning I provide medical nutrition therapy. My specialty area is instructing diabetes patients how to maintain, cope, and improve their condition through proper nutrition—it's a job that's close to my heart since my mother struggled with diabetes for years. I love my job because it's about forming relationships and motivating a long-term journey toward health. I see people with grim faces, and it's my job to give them hope and show them the way. One of my diabetes patients, after two months of exercise and diet change, came to me beaming and said, "This is the first day in fifteen years that I'm not obese, and it's a great feeling."

Food for Thought

Can we agree that Americans need a diet change? More than 60% of American adults are overweight or obese—that's an epidemic, and a ridiculous amount of health problems are nutrition related... think heart attacks, strokes, high blood pressure, diabetes, etc. Let's start thinking about food as fuel, being kind to our bodies, and saving some money on healthcare.

Skills

If you can't get along with somebody, they won't listen to your advice either—people skills are key. You also need to be organized and analytical—identifying a problem is just as difficult as managing it. Speaking skills are a real asset too. The most effective tools I have are information and explanation—people need to know the facts.

Education

I worked my way through college, and eventually earned the required Bachelor's degree in Food and Nutrition Sciences. Following college, I took on an internship and got several hundred hours of on-the-job training, which is priceless, trust me. Most people don't know it, but many states require licenses, one of the most prominent certifications being the Registered Dietician (RD). Also, you don't have to be a clinical dietician. This field is wide open—you could be a management dietician in a hospital or a food corporation like Kellogg, or you could be a community dietician working with pregnant women, in public health clinics, or with a Health Maintenance Organization (HMO).

Financial Factor

A fat paycheck helps me put food on the table. Last year I made $56,000, a little more than the average, but I also get great insurance and healthcare benefits that make my total compensation much higher.

If I Could Go Back

I would have kept in better contact with the people I grew up with—teachers, friends, professional contacts. You know, networking can start anytime, even from a small town setting. You never know who you'll need to call on. Keep your contacts close!

Projects

School and work are much alike in that both are just a series of "projects." Some projects are routine and repetitious. You probably have a set pattern to take care of them and get them out of the way as fast as possible. Others are more complex. At work, you'll have many projects to juggle; get good at it.

Learn how to recognize a project and how to handle one. What is a project? It's just about anything that you can't do immediately in a pre-set way.

What if I had asked *you* to write this book for me? That's quite a project. Would you know how to handle it? Here are a few tips:

•Be sure you know *exactly* what the project is. Do I mean write the book completely to the final draft, or just a rough draft I can take from there?

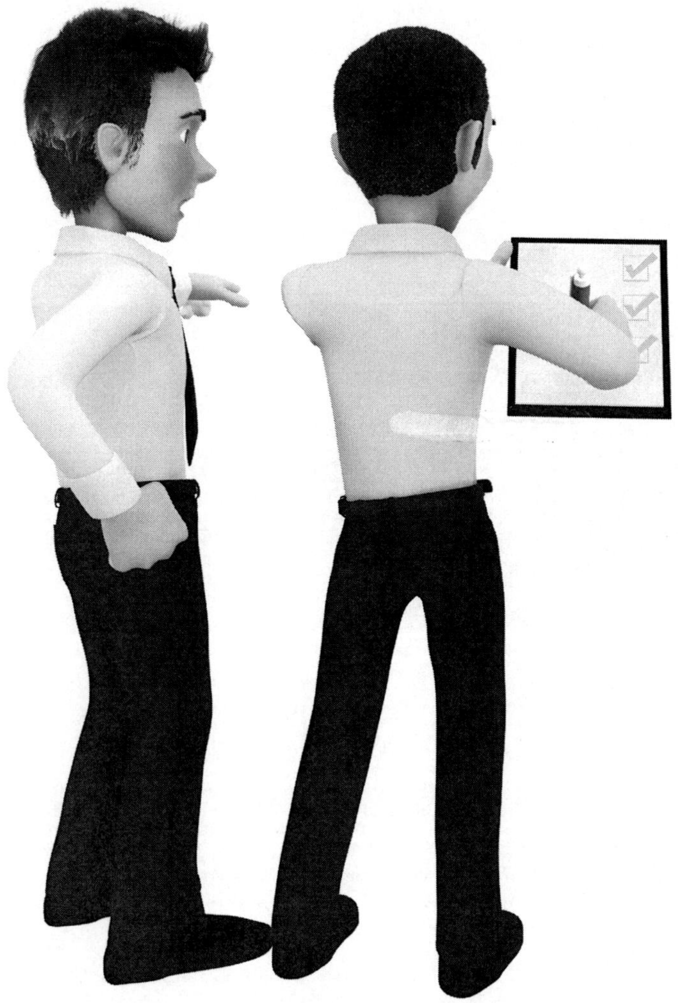

•What's the deadline? (*Yesterday* is the standard answer in the business world, and no one's kidding.) Do you want it perfect—all the typeset and art in, printed and bound? Or is "quick and dirty"—a rough mock-up—OK for now?

•Don't run off and complete a project without asking questions, so you'll look smart or cool. Most projects have go/no-go points and other interim decisions to be made. That's what teamwork is, even though usually only one person is responsible for the project being done on time and in budget.

Become the person who can do that.

Job Title: 3-D Animation Wizard

Success

One of the things that inspires me most is just watching people interact. Sounds creepy, but when I was younger, I was a computer geek—people called me Oz because I looked like Ozzy Osbourne's long-lost child, so I spent a lot of time watching people who didn't know they were being watched. I hated not being understood, but I learned a lot about movements, speech motions, and especially body language. My fantasy was to work with Tim Burton on a movie like *Corpse Bride*. The animation was just like whoa! So I took those computer skills and went to work. I graduated and I got my start doing character rigging for CG characters in TV commercials. A director saw my work and asked if I wanted to try animation. I said, "Yes ma'am, thank you," got nervous, and ran out of the room. Where am I working now? DreamWorks. Be jealous.

"Reel" Life

In movies and video games, motion-capture technology is changing everything. Actors like Andy Serkis (He's the actor behind "Gollum" from *Lord of the Rings*) put on sensors that record every gesture and facial twitch. Then, animators like me make the 3-D character come to life for the final reel.

Skills

An understanding of anatomy, human emotions, and life sciences might not be obvious, but it's important. I hope you have the creative drive to succeed, and an understanding of art basics like line, shape, color, and form are essential to all artistic design. After that, applying your artistic talent is all in mastering technical tools like Maya rendering and After Effects.

Education

Your education can go from a technical certificate program to a Master's degree. I would suggest at least a Bachelor's degree, depending on what you want to animate. All the great artists, Renoir, Michelangelo, and da Vinci to name a few, studied hard and practiced hard to master their craft, and there's a learning curve to animation too, including all sorts of technical skills like bump-mapping, lighting and texture, rendering, choreography, cinematography, and so on. Bottom Line: A good portfolio is better than a degree. Collect the best material from your college experience for a demo-reel, and keep revising as you get better and better.

Financial Factor

Salary ranges from \$35,000–\$70,000 a year. Video game animators can make a lot more, up to a six-figure salary. I started at an unpaid internship and worked my way into that entry-level \$40,000/year rigging job. Not bad for a small town social outcast, right?

If I Could Go Back

Hard to say, I'm not sure I would change anything. I was an unhappy kid, but I ended up at DreamWorks doing my Dream Work—see what I did there? Oh, nothing changes—that's the kind of lame pun that got nasty notes put on my back in high school.

Portfolio

A "portfolio" is not just for artists.

A portfolio is merely an example of your work.
A portfolio need not be fancy, and should not be artificially fabricated.
A nice notebook or black pocket file is just fine.
Never underestimate the worth of a portfolio or the fact that YOU can have one.
Here are just a few kinds of possible portfolio items; shoot for quality, not quantity, and when you can, "show" instead of tell.

- Your own letterhead; let it reflect your personality.
  If you excel in auto mechanics, ink your treads and run over some paper; be creative!
  On this letterhead, introduce yourself and state why you are giving someone your portfolio.
- Your resume; one page is best; keep it short and sweet and honest. Be precise, not vague.
- Letters of recommendation: try to obtain these in real time, not later; be sure you make copies and don't give away the original. Someone may vouch for your morals, honesty, skills, talents, or other great attributes; if you "did good," they will be happy to say so.
- A business card is optional.
- Examples of your work: for example:
  If you're an artist, samples.
  If you're a photographer, photos.
  If you detail cars, show a shiny one!
  If you had a paper route, show you and a satisfied customer.
  If you worked in fast food, show a photo of you and your manager, all looking happy.
  Any awards.
  If you won an essay or some other writing or speaking competition, include a copy.
  If you designed something, show a sketch.
  If you were in ROTC, show a picture of you in your dress uniform.
  If you were in FHA and had a prize cow entry, well, moo-ya: show her!

All these items are not rote, token representations of anyone…they are a mirror reflection of the great person you are, and lets someone else see that at a glance. Just because you bothered, counts.

If it's neat and tidy, that counts double. If it's creative and clever, that counts triple. No typos, well, that's amazing!

Job Title: Diagnostic Medical Sonographer

Success

I'm the first in my family to ever go to college, so I thought, "go big or go home," and got on a medical track to be a surgeon. I wanted to wear the scrubs and yell about needing a scalpel. The first time I saw blood in an operation, I passed out and dropped to the floor—dreams crushed! As it turns out, radiology and sonography are some of the coolest technologies available in the medical field. I'm not a genius (the IQ tests told me so), but it's pretty simple, really. We use high-frequency sound waves to make images of the inside the body. I love interacting with patients and seeing them walk out of our offices on their way to better health. I think my most important diagnosis is the early stages of cancer. Catch it early and survival rates usually go up.

Cool Options

Being a diagnostic medical sonographer means that you can work in a lot of different specialty careers. For example, obstetric sonographers do ultrasounds for pregnant women to track fetus development; musculoskeletal sonographers image muscles, ligaments, and joints; and neurosonographers specialize in imaging the nervous system, including the brain. Not to mention, this career is expected to grow by 44% in ten years.

Skills

Other than technical skills, interpersonal skill might not be an obvious requirement. I work closely with patients who are often in extreme pain or mental distress. You need to be careful, detail-oriented and have good hand-eye coordination. At the end of the day, my feet are worn out from standing and assisting patients. You've got to have stamina!

Education

You can get either an Associate degree or a Bachelor's degree in sonography. I started out in radiology and easily transferred over. Depending on what you specialize in, you have to get licensed to practice. It's all about learning to diagnose properly using the equipment. Don't worry if you don't know what type of sonographer to be—going through school will help you decide and there's plenty of room to explore before you settle down.

Financial Factor

The average sonographer gets paid about \$60,000/year with a range of \$45,000–\$90,000/year. My family was never well off, and it was tough growing up. My mom was a bus driver and my father out of the picture, so it's really important to me to have financial peace of mind. I made \$72,000 last year and took my mom on her first vacation in 27 years.

If I Could Go Back

I wouldn't go back, because going back means going back to school. I was glad to get out of there and into an actual career. Besides, being a surgeon would have meant a long 12 years of training. No way! I did the least amount possible to get to this great career—although that anatomy course in high school probably would have been better than gym class.

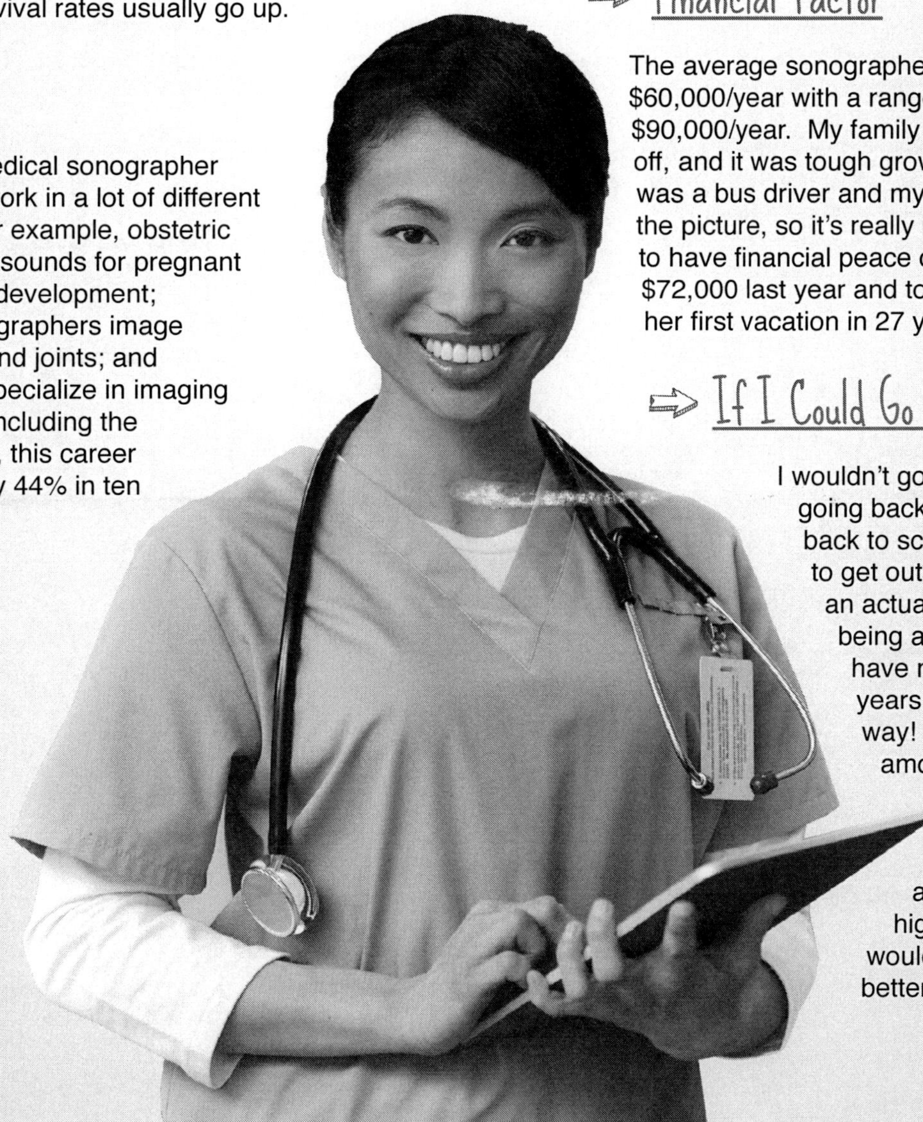

Don't Be a Prisoner

No matter what you're whining about, at least (hopefully) you are not in prison hoping to get a job someday. New criminal justice reform laws are being planned to emphasize classroom education and online job training for inmates.

Enhancing educational opportunities for nonviolent offenders is important. Juvenile prisoners still have a lot of life ahead, and having made a "mistake," most are eager to prepare for a better future.

Most of these inmates volunteer to participate in any type of instruction available to them. Of the 2,500–3,000 GED exams given to prisoners each year, about 74% pass. They then go on to vocational programs to gain skills in construction, maintenance, mechanics, and service industries.

So you see, you should quit whining about "how hard it is" and take advantage of your own advantages. Prisoners are. There is opportunity for everyone. Never let failure or setbacks determine your future. The only person who can really hold your future success hostage is you.

Opportunities multiply as they are seized.
—Sun Tzu

Job Title: International Social Worker

Success

People ask me "what do you do?" and I always joke, "I love people, it's my job," but that really might be the best summary. It started during summer in high school when my mom rounded up my sister and me for a church mission trip to South Africa. I packed a suitcase full of my favorite clothes, and when we got to the slums outside of Johannesburg, my mother said, "Now I want you to take all of those clothes you brought and give them away." I was confused at first, angry at my mother, but when handing over my Converses, I understood what a pair of shoes really means to kid who's never had any. I waited several years to go to college—tried my hand at freelance writing, but when I heard about social work, everything clicked. Now I'm an anti-trafficking international social worker. For five years now, I've been living in Cambodia, rehabilitating human trafficking victims while educating children and teachers about ways to avoid becoming a human slave. Believe it or not, slavery still exists in every major city in the U.S., not just in Europe like in the movie *Taken.*

Who We Are

Change comes one-on-one: We are youth counselors in schools. We are working with juvenile delinquents for a better future. We are caring for abused women seeking shelter. Change comes large-scale: We change laws so people will be treated fairly and humanely, working in churches, humanitarian organizations, and non-profit groups around the world.

Skills

This isn't for everyone. You need a big heart with lots of compassion, people skills, and a genuine empathy for others. Organization is priority—rather, helping someone else organize is key. Whether working for Child Protection Services or in a psychiatric ward, have patience, because a social worker's job is never finished.

Education

Even if you love and care about people, knowing HOW to love and care for people requires training. Entry-level social work jobs require a Bachelor's degree, and many clinical jobs require completing a Master's of Social Work (MSW) program, which usually runs for two years. There's a lot of misplaced love in the world—learn how to put yours to good use!

Financial Factor

Social work isn't the high-life of fame and excess, but we earn a decent living with a salary range of $35,000–$50,000/ year.

If I Could Go Back

Many women from Eastern Europe, Russia, and Asian countries like Laos and Thailand are sex slaves in massage parlors and brothel rings. Students from my university held an educational conference that pressured law enforcement to put an end to the sex-parlors near our school. I'm living in Cambodia, but if I could go back to the United States, I would help end sex-trafficking in ALL U.S. cities.

Slouching Toward Success

First, do like your mom says and never slouch!

Then again, beware Mom…and Dad, for that matter.

Huh? Just thinking aloud here, but if you have fabulous parents who never let you fail, excel in self-esteeming you, dole out cash instead of letting you earn your own, make decisions for you (including those you should make yourself), wash your clothes/cook your meals/clean your room, pay for your car/insurance/gas…well, keep them! Keep them, yes, but, really, you know when it's time to stand on your own two feet. You started that back when you learned to walk, so don't revert to crawling now.

Let's see, how can I say this: Grow up, get off the sofa/phone/computer, check your ego, and anything else that you are letting hinder you from transcending to adulthood. Kids who have it tough don't usually have these "unfortunate" issues, but if you feel in your smart heart of hearts that one day you will be one of those so-called "adults" who return home to live with their parents, then STOP, THINK, CHANGE.

Good tips include getting a part-time job, taking responsibility for ALL your personal business whether that's making a dentist appointment or ironing your shirts. School—*all* that is up to you.

You are only entitled to what you accomplish, only as confident as you are competent, and only as free as you don't free-load. All kidding aside, you can later "blame" your parents for holding you back by doing everything for you, enabling you to be a kid long after you aren't, and anything else you want to lay at their (and perhaps still your) doorstep.

You don't want to do this. You want to grow up. It's a process, not something that happens when you get handed your diploma. Parents are well-intentioned. But there are reasons that sometimes, less coddled, less pampered, less well-heeled or helped kids go on to zoom right past their spoiled peers.

I think that's where that "she or he who laughs last laughs best" expression comes from?

⇨ Don't fail to launch. It's fun at the right time, but not soooooo much later on.

Note: Of course many hard-working young adults fall on hard times and return home. That's different. You know the difference.

Job Title: Religious Activities Director

Success

I'm the organizational director for a small denomination in my town, and my career is the love of my life! I'm involved in so many people's lives and get to be a helping joy to the parents and students in our congregation. I plan, organize, and direct the educational programs we do in our congregation including themed luncheons, community outreach, and religious study groups. My favorite thing is to plan charity events and mission trips. I love being creative and finding fun ways to involve our members, young and old.

Innovation

I believe our community shouldn't be divided by religions. Lately, I've been listening to the news about the misunderstandings between Christians and Muslims in the United States. I got inspired and started a program to better educate our congregation about religious neighbors. We had a 4th of July potluck with a local Muslim mosque to share our communities and better understand each other. Who was it that said, "Love thy neighbor?"

Skills

You will need people skills, superior organization, and a lot of time to chat. If you feed off social interaction, being a Religious Activities Director is like being at a constant Sunday-brunch buffet. Knowledge of basic math and finances will help you keep the doors open for all.

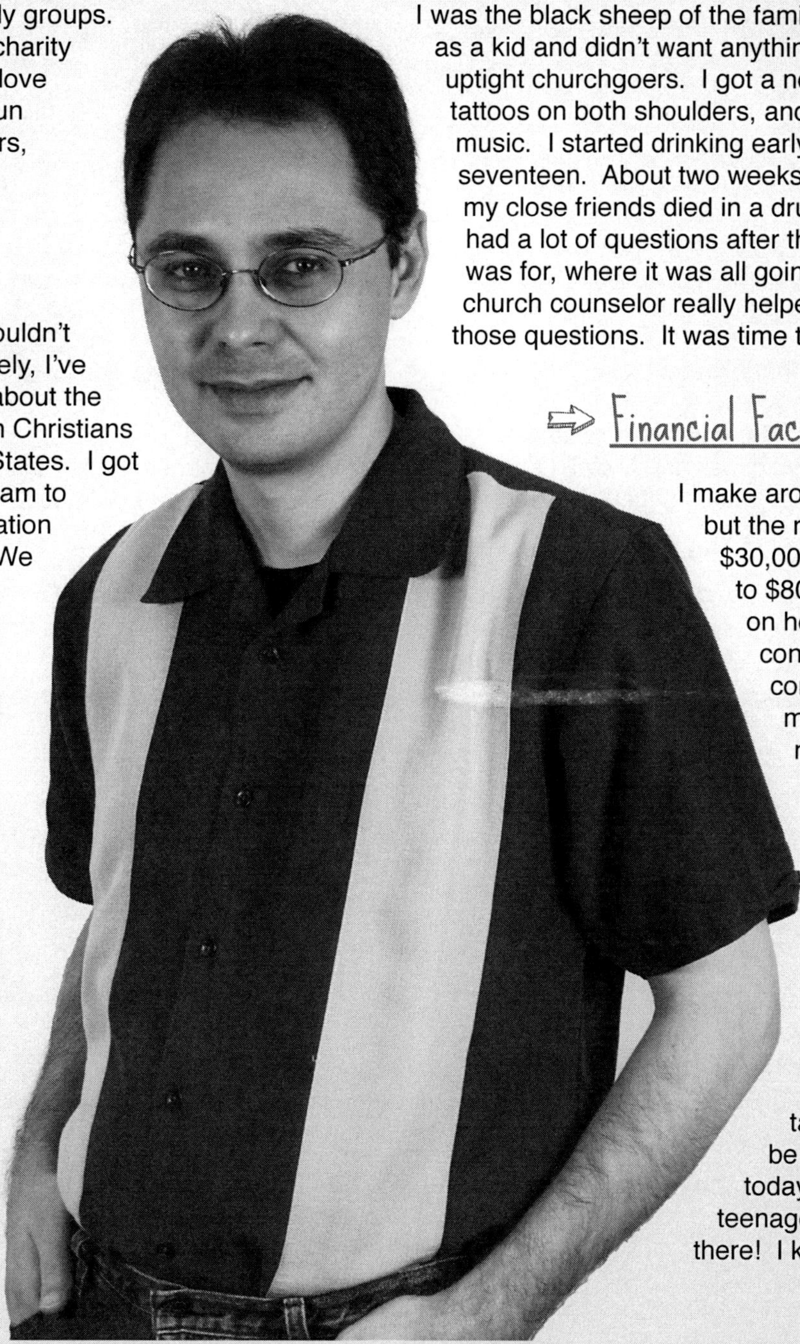

Education

Experience is the most important qualification. If you attend church, get involved, and have something to put on a resume. You can also major in religious studies in college—that will give you a great background of many different faiths. It's funny, because I grew up in the same church with the same congregation, but I didn't get what it was all about. My dad was the minister, and I was the black sheep of the family. I was rebellious as a kid and didn't want anything to do with the uptight churchgoers. I got a nose-ring at fourteen, tattoos on both shoulders, and listened to scream-o music. I started drinking early on and got a DUI at seventeen. About two weeks after that, three of my close friends died in a drunk-driving accident. I had a lot of questions after that, about what my life was for, where it was all going, and I found that my church counselor really helped me answer a lot of those questions. It was time to get involved again.

Financial Factor

I make around $40,000/year, but the range is more like $30,000/year all the way up to $80,000/year depending on how big your congregation is. I have a comfortable life, but for me it's rarely about the money.

If I Could Go Back

I kind of think that every road takes you somewhere for a reason. The mistakes I made taught me how to be the person I am today. I love working with teenagers because I've been there! I know how tough it is.

Ignorance Is No Excuse of...Ethics

One good reason to be a daily reader of news of the world and state is that the tempo of the legal part of business is always changing. There are always lawsuits, cases, judicial rulings, and other such things going on. You will learn a lot that you need to know by paying attention.

All states have a state ethics commission. Ethics is a big thing in the real world of work. You'll hear words such as transparency, loophole, advocate, lobbyist, and wonder what any of that could possibly have to do with you. It does.

Ethics is not a vague word; it means specific things. Pay attention to the rules of school, including college, your employee handbook, and anything that even looks halfway legal. You can be sure that the details either protect your rights or protect others against something you may do that is not ethical.

"Not me!" you insist. But the newspapers are full of stories of people who claimed, "I didn't know." Influence peddling, banned gifts, bribes, collusion—heck, who even knows for sure what these things are? Informed citizens do. Make it your point to be savvy about caring about things that really do affect you.

Maybe not today or tomorrow, but always—you not only want to be on the right side of the law, you might even help craft laws, uphold laws, communicate legal issues, be charged with looking out for the rights of employees, or employers, or animals, or...well, you get the picture.

Job Title: Interior Design Universal Designer

Success

Hi, I'm a universal designer. Never heard of it? This subfield of interior design didn't exist thirty years ago. Just like fashion, interior design is constantly changing, but universal design is here to stay. We believe a building's interior should be beautiful, innovative, and most of all functional, so all people, young and old, can enjoy convenient indoor environments. I love it because I get to be fashionable, choose color schemes and use my knowledge of space, but it's also about being practical, understanding what frustrates people, and what can be done smarter and quicker. It's true—beauty is about what's on the inside.

The Insiders

Interior design jobs can be very different. Look at "sustainable design," which is needed for energy-efficient buildings. Kitchen and bath designers can help you remodel the spaces you use most, and light designers know all about lighting for offices, homes, and public spaces. It's a great place to be if you're creative and practical. I've really enjoyed sprucing up businesses around my hometown.

Skills

I'm a people-person on all levels from start to finish. I interact with architects, city planners, and individual clients in a big group effort to get any design project completed. I'm a detail fanatic, and nothing goes unnoticed or unattended. I usually have artistic visions for a project—my favorite part is closing my eyes and imagining all the possibilities. Remodeling a space is like bringing a piece of art to life, livable art, that is.

Education

College took me longer than four years, being a single parent going back to school, but I finally got my Bachelor's degree. Most design jobs require at least a Bachelor's, and now that my girl is a little older, I'd like to go for my Master's. All interior designers have to be licensed by the state and certified by nationally approved programs. You'll be taking art classes as well as business essentials and computer-aided design courses.

Financial Factor

I made $42,000 last year working for an architectural design company. The average interior designer makes around $46,000/year. Some are self-employed, but going that route means having a 24/7 job. I prefer working a job with decent hours and good benefits.

If I Could Go Back

I know I'm a hard worker, but sometimes I think I made it harder on myself, like I needed to prove to my parents that I could do something on my own and be successful. I'm glad I did it that way, putting myself through school, but maybe I wouldn't be so afraid to ask for help now and then. I was even too proud to talk to my high school counselor about what job I might want to do.

Gotta Milk Those Cows!

It was the most unusual "talk" I ever gave. I'd been invited to speak to parents of top-drawer high school students in the Raleigh Durham/Chapel Hill, North Carolina area, land of high IQs and higher salaries. It was contentious from the start, unusual since I'm just a kids' book writer, you know?

It was a stormy night, and the parents seemed ill at ease and ornery. I had no idea why until they began to grouse. Most worked in the Research Triangle at high tech jobs; many had just been laid off. Many, I learned, were losing their homes, being forced into bankruptcy. There was a look of panic on their faces and a general dismay palpable in the room. And still, good parents, they had come to hear me speak. Because I knew their kids were gifted, I was sort of tough on them. The *Challenger* had just exploded in the sky and there was all that talk about something called O-rings. I was talking about responsibility, owning a problem, speaking up…those sorts of things, when all heck broke loose. "Our kids shouldn't be expected to do those things!" one father insisted.

"Then who should?" I asked, thinking that if not their gifted kids to handle oversight, integrity, ambiguity, and them the best and brightest, why not?

Their ire instantly turned in a surprising direction. They seemed to want to talk about how their sons would have to move away and change schools, right in the middle of football season. ("Priorities?" I thought to myself.) Maybe I missed something while I was musing, but suddenly a mother stood up and accosted a family sitting to the side. It was clear that this family was not One of Them. No three-piece suits and skinny ties; no Lily Pulitzer sundresses. "SHE won't even let her sons stay after school for football practice!" the woman screeched.

I noted the three well-built young men sitting beside their mother, the only "kids" in the audience. The complaining woman continued, "We want our kids to get college scholarships ('In football?,' I'm now wondering in amazement?) and those boys are dragging the team down by going home first and only coming back later for practice!" It was clear that these boys were football scholarship material. The accosted mother stood up. She was near tears. "You don't understand!" she said. "We have to milk the cows!" There were insulting giggles and smirks from the other parents.

One of her sons stood up. In as polite a tone as I imagine he found possible, he said, "Ma'am, you don't understand. We have to go home first and milk the cows. Our family's dairy is our business. The cows have to be milked. The cows come first. Football comes second." He sat back down, and except for the outside growl of the storm, the room was quiet.

Truly, I felt as if I had been transported to another time and place. How was it that the "smart ones in the room" had missed out on the "real world" skills of not living beyond your means, having emergency savings, and teaching their children a certain kind of responsibility?

The parents had assured me earlier that "No, of course none of our kids work after school!" The young dairyman had just trumped all their kids by spitting out an entire business education in a few words: "The cows come first."

How, I wondered, can we not forget that even our best and brightest can come to the work table clueless about the real world and hindered by a lack of certain work skills, attitudes, and understandings? If all the parents' kids had also been in the room, and I were hiring, I already knew who my top picks would be.

Job Title: Neonatology Nurse

Success

I won't bore you with baby talk. I hear enough of it at work from parents and my coworkers—"Isn't he precious? Oh, just look at those tiny fingers and teeny-weeny toes!" It's nice, but not all baby-care is goo-goo and giggles. I'm an RN (Registered Nurse) specializing in caring for newborn babies, and let me tell you, some babies are a real miracle. Last month we monitored a baby who was born at 24 weeks, that's three months premature—she only weighed 1 pound, 6 ounces! I was one of the nurses who monitored her progress to health, secured intravenous therapy, and checked for birth defects. Sometimes I forget that my job is special, but when we hand over a healthy baby to its parents—that's a great feeling.

Opportunities

A nursing degree and RN certification will open doors to work in places like emergency rooms (ER), intensive care units (ICU), or operating rooms (OR)—or maybe you'll work in a pediatric office, or perhaps you want to do in-home visits. Really, registered nurses are in high demand, and it's only expected to increase!

Skills

I guess most of what you need is technical training, but nurses have other qualities too, like clear communication with patients—bilingual skills are highly valuable. My patients and their families expect me to be compassionate and emotionally stable—no breakdowns here! In the work area, you need to be detail-oriented and organized. Sharpen those critical thinking skills, and keep in mind you can't be queasy around blood, guts, or poop.

Education

I got my Associate degree in nursing in only two years followed by getting a license through state certification and a national certification program. Some employers, depending on your type of work, will require extra certification through a professional organization. You can also earn a Bachelor's degree in nursing, say, if you want the four-year college experience. After getting licensed, I worked as a staff nurse in a neonatal clinic, and then got certified as a neonatology nurse. I really like having upward mobility. "What's that?" you ask? Upward mobility is advancement! Next year, I'm getting qualified to be a Neonatal Nurse Practitioner.

Financial Factor

Registered nurses make good money—average is $65,000/year, but you might start off, like me, around $35,000, from lacking experience. The more you specialize or become better qualified, the more opportunities you'll have to make closer to $80,000/year.

If I Could Go Back

I've always had a romantic idea of being my own boss, with a nice bed and breakfast inn in the mountains. I've never felt confident enough about my math skills or business knowledge to chase that dream.

Details

I live in a land of details—hundreds, thousands of them, often in a single day.

Details matter…a lot. If you don't think so, remember the *Challenger*; they were just O-rings, right?

No matter what you study in school during the remainder of your education (uh, that would be from now on) it will include lots of details. Are you good at handling them? If not, get good.

Job training may be done on an individual basis or as a group. The trainer will be watching for the person who is good at details: knowing that the one and the zero matter; using the right screw; knowing the correct order of the process—everything.

Every job you ever have will include endless details to learn, assess, tweak, or otherwise manipulate. That requires focus, attention, and intention. You suffer when someone does not pay attention to details. Ever had a "lemon" car…a screwed-up pizza order…a "We're sorry we misplaced your scholarship application"? Let's not even think about having the wrong leg amputated, or some other "Houston, we have a PROBLEM!" scenario.

At least I only deal in words, so what's a typo or two? Let me just say that when I come to a fork in the writing road, I ALWAYS check the spelling, 'cause I've had some close calls with disaster that might have meant a million-dollar reprint—out of my pocket.

The devil is in the details, indeed. Practice nailing details; it's a good habit and a great skill and separates the men from boys and girls from women and hired from fired in the real world workplace.

Job Title: Military Intelligence Specialist

Success

I can't tell you I'm James Bond or that I'm responsible for ending the Cold War, but what I CAN say is just as important. Military intelligence protects our soldiers and secures national defense. I'm trained to collect, decipher, and analyze foreign communications, intercepted messages, and cultural signals. One person could drown in the oceans of data—we are only as capable as the members of our team, including geospatial imagists, interpreters and translators, intelligence officers, and other military commanders who handle high-tech, CLASSIFIED information. Recently, we've reduced the number of U.S. deaths by Afghani improvised explosive devices (IEDs) by choking off the supply of fertilizer used to make homemade bombs—that's what it's all about.

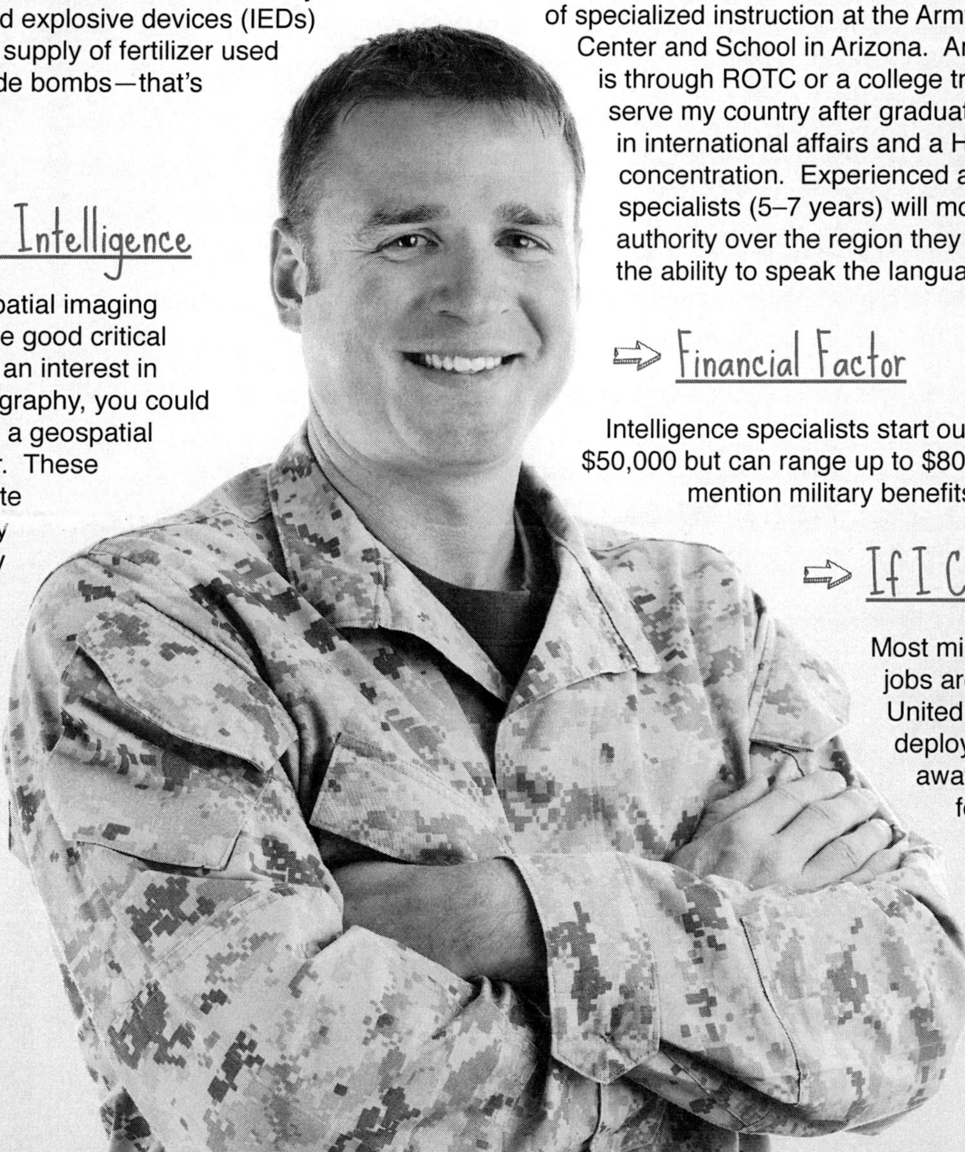

Geospatial Intelligence

I mentioned geospatial imaging before. If you have good critical thinking skills and an interest in technology or geography, you could be a candidate for a geospatial intelligence career. These professionals locate and assess enemy terrain and military targets using satellite imaging and advanced electronic mapping. It's a cool career.

Skills

Do you love computers, studying information, or reading about foreign cultures? If not, an intelligence specialist job is not for you. Being trustworthy is valuable—leaking information is a fast track to military court. You also need strong communication skills, excellent writing and reading comprehension, and the ability to organize information. Don't worry if you're not a pro at all of those things. The military hires potential—we can make you great!

Education

Necessities: A high school diploma in hand and at least a 105 on the skilled technical version of the Armed Services Vocational Aptitude Battery test. If you survive nine weeks of basic training, you'll move on to 83 days of specialized instruction at the Army Intelligence Center and School in Arizona. Another way to go is through ROTC or a college track. I choose to serve my country after graduating with a degree in international affairs and a Hebrew linguistic concentration. Experienced analysts and specialists (5–7 years) will most likely be an authority over the region they cover, including the ability to speak the language.

Financial Factor

Intelligence specialists start out at around $50,000 but can range up to $80,000/year, not to mention military benefits.

If I Could Go Back

Most military intelligence jobs are located in the United States, but I was deployed. I've been away from my family for almost a year, and there's no way to describe that separation. I hope to be relocated closer to home.

Slippery Slope

In business, there's this thing called a "slippery slope." It's not for skiing or water sliding. It's not for staying on, even though we all spend some time on the slippery slope.

Here are just a few examples of slippery slopes:

- You are getting along fine in school (you thought), then discover you are short a course or failed an exam and suddenly you are not continuing on your planned upward course; what do you do?
- You are in college and run out of money; it's work or add to your debt—how do you decide this slippery slope situation?
- You're in a great certificate course and just a few hours from finishing when your mom gets sick and the family needs you to come home. The employer holding a job for you says he just can't; what do you do?
- You start your own business and your best account goes bankrupt without paying you. That was the money to get you over the hump of the slippery slope to profit and success. What do you do now?

Most slippery slopes actually don't go straight down. They look a lot more like a Marine Corps obstacle course filled with a wild array of one impossible challenge after the other. No matter, it's your job to get up and over, down, around, and through. If you survive, you usually thrive. If you don't, well, it's back down that dadgum slippery slope to start over yet again! Learn to survive, outsmart, and even avoid the slippery slopes; it can be done.

Anticipate, plan, have backups, have backups to your backups.

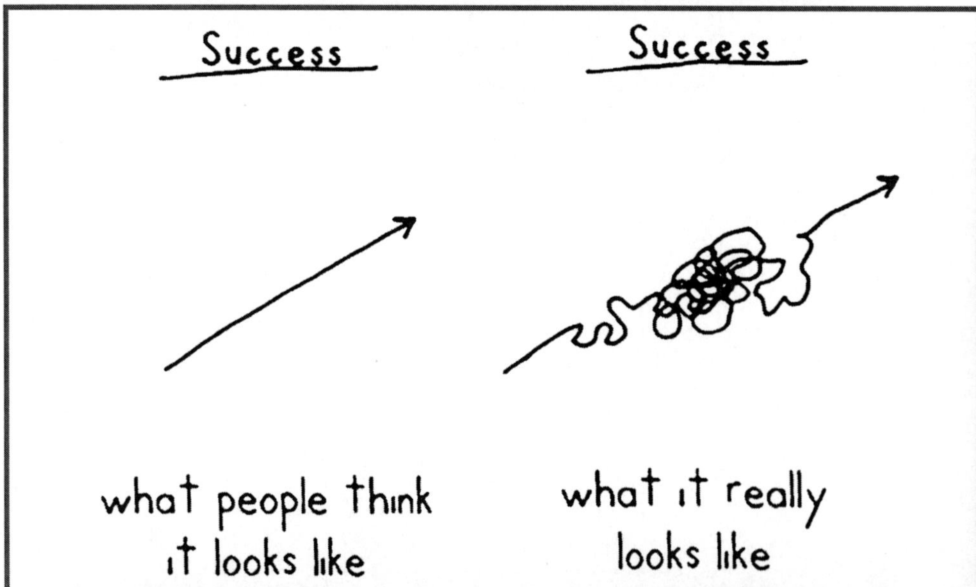

Job Title: Funeral Director

Success

I was not a strange child. I didn't bury my stuffed animals in the backyard. Actually, I don't remember knowing what death even was. I wanted to be a theater actor, and then an astronaut, and then a web-designer. It was after my sister's funeral that I considered it—the funeral director was so caring and compassionate to our family in our time of need. With guidance from her, I took on an apprenticeship, got my Associate degree, and went through certification. Now, I oversee all the preparations for a funeral home, from embalming or cremation to the dressing and cosmetic application. Working with the families is my favorite part. Each family has a different character and history—lots of striking personalities. And it's not all gloom and doom—humor is the best shield against sadness. Just recently, my colleague's car was stolen with cremated ashes still in the trunk, awaiting delivery. When I fessed up to the family, one of the men said, "Nobody even liked Aunt Camilla and now somebody went and stole her."

The Job that Never Dies

Always count on death and taxes—people always die, meaning the job market for funeral directors never dies, although the ways funerals are conducted might change in the future. What do you think about your remains being shot up on a rocket into space?

Skills

The family always comes first—their wants, needs, and their time—so I'd say people skills are the biggest part of this business. You need to understand that is not always timely, but that time management is crucial to effective funeral procedures. The most difficult part is the emotional side, dealing with grief on a daily basis. Bring tissues.

Education

Most mortuaries used to be family businesses, but now that's not so true. An Associate degree in mortuary science is required, however, a growing number of employers require a Bachelor's degree. My Associate program included courses in ethics, funeral services, and grief counseling as well as business law—the weirdest thing I learned was embalming. Licensed funeral directors must complete one to three years' apprenticeship under the supervision of an experienced mortician. On-the-job training is really the best.

Financial Factor

A good funeral director, like myself, makes around $50,000/year. Most people think funeral directors are putting money in the bank every day—people are always dying right? Actually death rates have slowed because of better healthcare, but with good business skills, you can still make a decent living.

If I Could Go Back

I would have dyed my hair crazy colors in high school. Now that I'm a funeral director, I am expected to be conservative and traditional. It goes with the solemn and religious professionalism of my job.

The Buffalo Jump

What's it like out there in the real world of jobs and careers? Some say it's like a buffalo jump. Native Americans once lured buffalo over a cliff, in order to kill a lot of them at one time.

Now, I don't mean it's that bad out there! But if you run with the herd, you could wind up over the jump. It's fine in high school to be one of the crowd, to fit in. By the time you head off to more schooling or a new job, it's time to be your own person. In the real work world, employees look at individual ability, achievement, and performance.

You create value to your employer by being truly willing, able, and valuable—able to listen, learn, and achieve results. You do not have to be a leader; where would Steve Jobs have been without the quiet, shy "Woz" who figured out how to build a personal computer? If you're a follower, be a Woz, and you'll be just as valuable as your leader. (They split the Apple stock 50/50, you know.)

A group mentality is often deadly in the workplace. Remember, there are no rules. The person who can "bring it" can zoom on ahead of others in spite of their age, seniority, or job title. Even a lateral move is a sort of promotion; YOU have been chosen to learn another role in the company.

It's fine to have friends at work; it's comforting and rewarding. But save that for lunch. In the meantime, if you want to move ahead, stand on your own, and don't worry about "showing up" anyone else with your smarts, skills, or willingness to work hard or long.

There are always some buffalo that don't fall for the jump over the cliff!

Job Title: Surgical Tech

Success

Surgeons aren't the only people in an operating room. A healthcare team takes a lot of different people, you know, physicians and surgeons, registered nurses, and surgical technicians like me. I don't care to be the boss of an operation, but I do my job well. That means preparing patients for their operations, making sure the operating room is clean and properly equipped, and passing dangerous instruments to a surgeon during sensitive operations. It's an exciting job, and I'm just as necessary as anybody else. In fact, doing my job well means everyone stays safe from infection or mishap—I mean, I'll make sure an instrument like a knife or tube isn't left inside you after everything's stitched up. Deal?

Keys to Success

The first key to being a successful surgical technologist is to know your instruments. There are a lot of medical instruments in an operating room. You need to stay up to date on all the common names and any new instruments in the hospital. Second key—know the procedure. What is the third key? Know the doctor you're working for, what instruments he or she likes to use, and how he or she likes to run procedures. Doctors can be demanding, so get to know their needs fast.

Skills

Memorization skills and strong mental checklists separate the prepared surgical tech from the...well, the unprepared tech without a job. Being clumsy is a recipe for disaster in this job, and hopefully you can handle a little bit of stress...okay, maybe a lot of stress. Also, don't get too comfortable, because you'll be on your feet a lot.

Education

Start with high school science courses like health, biology, and chemistry. Do they still require math in high school? Take that too. Getting your high school diploma will let you into a community or vocational college. You can get a certification or Associate degree in Surgical Technology in two years max. After that, it's about working your way into the right workplace. I worked in a hospital operating room, for a while, but decided a quieter, private setting suits me just fine. Now I'm working for a plastic surgeon.

Financial Factor

I get paid $42,000/year, which is about average, but really I get a lot of awesome benefits, like healthcare insurance, paid time off, reimbursed education, sick days and bonuses. Those benefits make my total compensation closer to $60,000!

If I Could Go Back

I think as a kid I destroyed my attention span. I watched TV a lot and then cell phones and everything else just made me a little distracted. It's really important to stay focused at a job, especially one like mine. I've trained myself to stay attentive, but there are ways to practice when you're younger. Try reading a book.

Walk Fast

Walk fast—sounds silly, doesn't it? But my daughter, Michele, president of our publishing company will not hire anyone who walks slow. When she greets a job candidate, shakes hands, then turns to lead them to her office for an interview…if she looks around and they are dragging far behind her, well, she just turns around, thanks them for their time, and marches them right back out the front door!

When I asked her why she did this, she said, "I figure if they can't hustle enough to get to my office, they will just drag their feet even more once they get the job. I walk fast and work fast and don't have time for worker slow-pokes."

Well, I guess you thought you could always figure out why you didn't get a job, right? If Steven Spielberg calls me into his office to talk about turning one of my books into a movie—I am gonna WALK FAST!

Job Title: Geotechnical Engineer

Success

Co-workers call me a "soil scientist," because I'm always talking about the ground. As a kid, I was all over construction sites with my dad, and I loved the big dump trucks and bulldozers, but I'm in a different part of that business now. I'm a civil engineer specializing in geology. I look at the ways large construction sites interact with the rock and soil. Geotechnical Engineers focus on the ground that supports major structures like highways, buildings, and bridges. I like seeing my work go from drawings on a page to something useful. And I can say I do my job well, and I enjoy it, but I don't let it take over my life. There's more important stuff out there. A great career is only one part of a healthy life.

Civil Engineering Wonders

Some true world wonders are civil engineering masterpieces—the Panama Canal and the Golden Gate Bridge, to name two American icons. The Channel Tunnel between England and France, traveling 50 kilometers in length under water, is the largest engineering project in the history of humanity. Just let us sit around and chat for a while, and we'll think of the next BIG thing.

Skills

A thing you might not think of…writing… it's beyond important. You'll be writing reports, proposals, and project plans. I face some pretty complex problems—lots of this job is scratching my head and trying different ideas. I'm a leader, but I know when to back out—it's a collaboration thing, so being a team player gets the job done. Also, I wouldn't have survived day one without my high school math skills.

Education

I hated school, but look at me, I made it! A four-year Bachelor's degree in Civil Engineering, national certification, state licensing, and an internship got me to where I wanted to be. I had to really develop my crummy writing skills in college, but I'm glad I did, because it paid off. I wanted to skip every English class I ever had, but I reckon it did me some good.

Financial Factor

Don't bring work home with you, but take home a nice salary. Civil engineers make an average of $77,000/year. I started out with a paid internship and landed an entry-level position at $50,000 to start. That's more than some jobs make, period.

If I Could Go Back

I use analytical math skills every day. I literally would have memorized my high school geometry book. Business management classes could have helped too. I actually played soccer in college, which helped give me the sense of teamwork I need as a manager.

Bob Scott

One of my favorite success stories is that of Bob Scott. He is the author of *God is My Co-Pilot.* A smart, sort of smart-alecky guy, he was a World War II flying ace, among many other things. But that's not what fascinates me about him.

After he achieved all his military goals, he baked 1,200 "healthy" oatmeal cookies to eat as he walked the entire Great Wall of China! When Bob Scott set his mind to something, nothing was going to stop him!

A lot of times, we try to live off our past achievements. But you're only as good as what you did today, not yesterday. Got a high school degree? That's great, but that's just a start, not a sit-back-and relax finish. Got a scholarship? The same. Your certificate, BA, MBA, PhD, whatever—plan to keep moving on.

After I published my first book, I thought I could check that off my list and say, "Been there, done that." I did not plan for success. I did not expect kids to want more—a lot more—for a long time. You can always sit on your laurels: that great promotion, your first business trip to Europe, but why?

Keep the momentum going, always. The purpose of an education and a career is also to have some fun, achieve some goals, begin to be able to call some of the shots your way, to bake 1,000 cookies, to write a book, sail around the world, or go for a long walk.

Bob Scott died, but he showed us how to live.*

**Bob was born in Waynesboro, Georgia. At age 12, he built a glider and flew it off the roof of his house into a rose bush. He was an Eagle Scout, sailed around the world as a deckhand after high school, graduated from West Point, taught fighter pilots, flew over Mt. Everest, was a decorated WWII hero, toured Europe by motorcycle, flew air mail in an open-cockpit, and, oh, many other things.*

The quality, not the longevity, of one's life is what is important.

—Martin Luther King, Jr.

Job Title: Foreign Service Officer

Success

There's a life out there bigger than yourself; you just have to seek it out. I was born in Libya to missionary parents, but I say I'm from West Virginia—I lived there long enough. I never thought I'd end up being a foreign diplomat to China, but it's a career that enriches and fulfills my life—something a nine-to-five job never gave me. In fact, sometimes it's an around-the-clock job issuing visas, protecting American citizens, and accompanying foreign officials on diplomatic matters, but I love experiencing culture, tasting exotic foods, and meeting fascinating people. It's great job satisfaction to represent my country at the U.S. Embassy in Beijing, while having the opportunity of a lifetime to live in a foreign country.

Culture Shock

All cultures are the same, but different. For example, tasting the local cuisine is one of the best ways to experience a foreign country—and sometimes the most stomach-turning. At a dinner with local Chinese public officials, I was shocked when the main entrée turned out to be monkey brains.

Skills

My main responsibility is handling reports—proofreading, assembling, and reviewing information consumes about half my time. Reading and writing are two of the best skills any employee can have, but it's an absolute "must have" for this job. Speaking that foreign language is "optional mandatory"...meaning, learn the language! Other qualities that will help you succeed are the desire to help others, the ability to engage in public discussion, and a passion to broaden your cultural horizons.

Education

You don't need a college degree, but higher education will get you a better starting position and better prepare you for the strain of writing and reviewing reports. If you sign up, the U.S. State Department gives several oral and written exams to test your communication skills. Not knowing what I wanted to do after college, a mentor of mine suggested a program teaching English to public schoolteachers in China. Stepping into that plane to China to teach abroad and live in that culture was the most difficult decision I've ever made—and I didn't realize it would lead to a great career. I returned to the U.S., worked retail and community service jobs off and on, and studied Mandarin Chinese in my spare time. My life wasn't going anywhere, and I wanted something more, something greater. Since I had Chinese language and writing skills, I took the tests and got a good entry-level job as a Foreign Service Officer.

Financial Factor

Starting salaries can range all the way from $30,000/year to $120,000/year depending on your education level and qualifying experience. Because I had prior language skills and a year's experience in China, my starting salary was $40,000/year—but I got raises!

If I Could Go Back

I would have gotten a public service degree instead of a history degree. I enjoyed the college experience and it gave me good study skills, but I hated paying back loans.

Ignorance is No Excuse of... ETIQUETTE

Huh? Yes, business etiquette is something you have to be concerned about. There's ordinary stuff, of course, like basic courtesy. If you have been a "please," "thank-you," "yes ma'am," "no sir" kind of kid all these years, you are in good shape. Otherwise, hmmm, better get a basic paperback etiquette book and catch up.

Among your peers, you can be as cool and quirky as you want. In most business scenarios, this is not so. It's the principle of the thing. I try to dress and act appropriately in the office, and certainly when representing my company out of the office, no matter how I like to dress and talk much more informally at home. It's just respect, good manners, and playing it safe. People do pay attention and care. They consider you an adult and are not apt to remind you, correct, or even frown. You'll just find that you've made yourself highly unwelcome, even out of a job. (No, I'm not kidding. Really!)

Good manners are just good sense. There are all kinds of folks in the workplace, not to mention the customer. It's your job to get along. A good way to do that is to be respectful in your dress, manner, speaking, and actions. No matter what you may think or someone else says, good manners have NOT gone out of style.

I love Ron Clark, a Disney Teacher of the Year.* He teaches even his youngest elementary students to have superlative manners, since he will be taking them out to dinner and out of the country.

I love to meet a plumber, or the guys in my warehouse, or anyone we might assume (falsely) to be the least likely to have good manners. They open the door for me, know how to introduce others, have a firm handshake, look me in the eye, can make conversation, say please and thank you and yes, ma'm. I am always so proud of them, appreciate them, and reward them every chance I get.

As a business owner, I must have great etiquette toward not only my customers, but also even the folks that I am a customer of; it's just smart business and the right thing to do.

In today's global work world, there are even more manners to learn, additional etiquette. So it's a lot easier if you have plain, old vanilla American manners down pat. You do, don't you?

Ron even had a movie made about his adventures as a world-class teacher—The Ron Clark Story** starring Matthew Perry as Ron.*

Job Title: Aircraft Launch and Recovery Specialist

Success

Hey, I'm happy you're listening! My job is to prepare the details of takeoff and landing by maintaining launch and recovery equipment. I also test visual landing aids and operate the emergency rescue equipment in case of a crash. Working for the military lets me see a different side of the world—I have nothing anchoring me down, and I like being deployed. I live on an aircraft carrier stationed off the coast of Italy, which means we get shore leave, provided all's quiet and peaceful. People say once military, always military, but when I get out of the service, I could pursue a career in air traffic control, but I'd rather go to college. It means a little extra schoolwork, but who knows what the future can hold?

Cool Gear

Fighter jets, cargo planes, and reconnaissance aircraft are my life. A typical aircraft carrier runway is only 1,000 feet long! That's 6,000 to 7,000 feet shorter than the average airport runway. We use catapults to launch fighter jets off the runway at speeds of 200 mph with engines at full throttle. It's truly an awesome experience!

Skills

You need to be comfortable working in dangerous spaces—attention to safety regulations can save your life and the lives of your crew. I know, it's quite an experience! Most of my work is hands-on, and I love working as part of a team. Oh! I also have a good understanding of mechanics and machine parts. Other than that, the military provides good training to its employees.

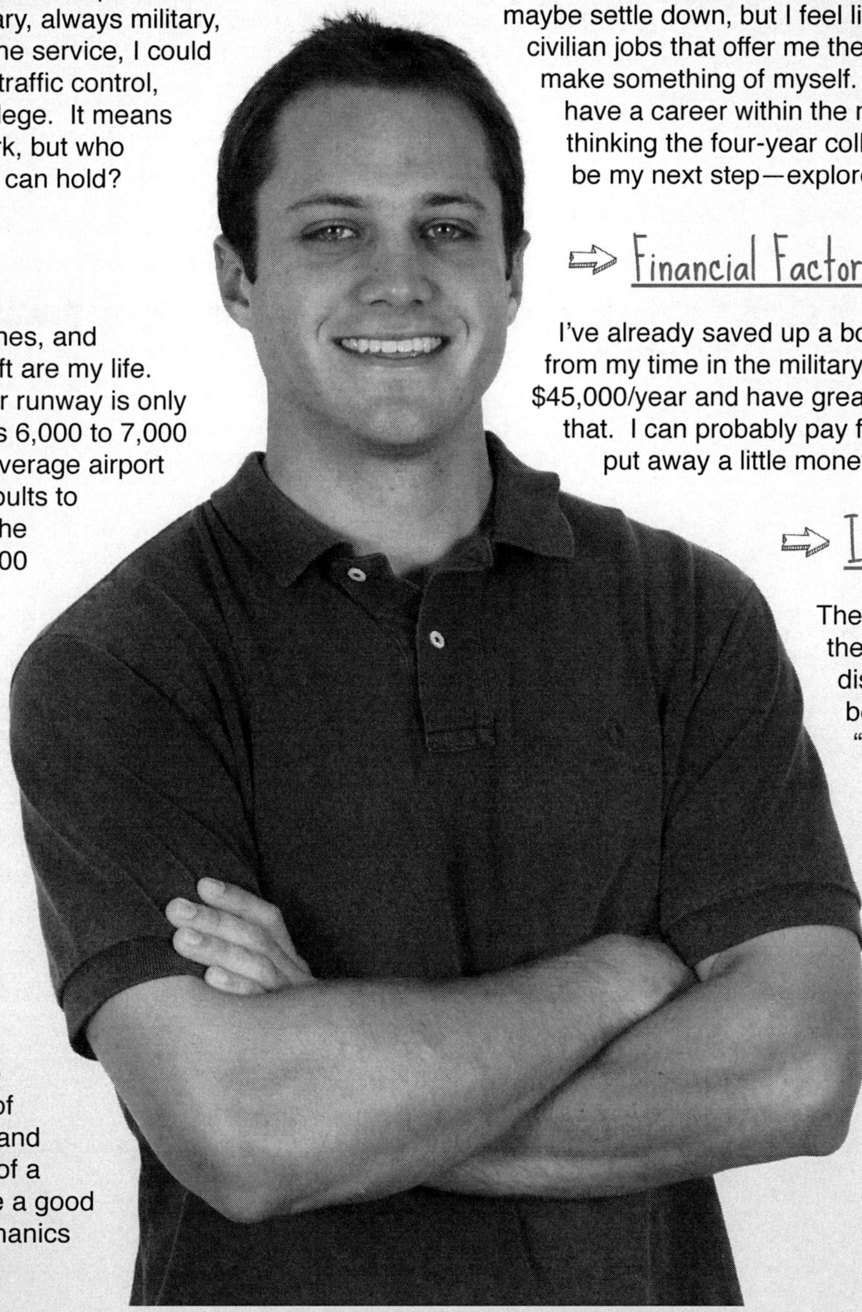

Education

I went into the Navy with only a high school diploma. I wanted to be an electrician, but I was assigned to work on the flight deck with a catapult crew. I liked repairing and maintaining the mechanical equipment so much, I requested extra training and was sent to classes in Philadelphia. I've been considering the civilian life, maybe settle down, but I feel like there aren't many civilian jobs that offer me the same opportunity to make something of myself. I could essentially have a career within the military, but I'm thinking the four-year college experience might be my next step—explore myself some more.

Financial Factor

I've already saved up a boatload of money from my time in the military. I'm making around $45,000/year and have great benefits on top of that. I can probably pay for college now and put away a little money for a rainy day.

If I Could Go Back

The military let me see the world. I wasn't a disciplined student, because I thought, "What does all this stuff matter to me?" The military straightened me out and trained me to do something useful. I should have been a better student back then, because education opens up worlds of possibility. I know that now.

College or Not?

College is a great thing. I sure hope my brain surgeon went there!

College (and any post-high school teaching place) is also a commodity, something you pay for. In many ways, it's not really much different from buying a home, car, furnishings, wardrobe, insurance, or other things of importance and value.

Some careers require college and lots of it. Others do not. Some jobs can be successfully obtained with a certificate, an apprenticeship, or through vocational school training, technical school, or community college.

Now, any of these places will be glad to take your money. That's how they stay in business. You do realize that, don't you? It's up to you to assess which pathway to further education is best for you. Today, even quality online classes are available; some colleges are offering three-year degrees to save you time and money. You get what you pay for. But often, paying top dollar is not only not necessary, it's not advisable. Discuss all this with your parents, best teacher, school career counselor, or other advisors that you trust.

A big mistake is to spend a lot of money for college if you don't want or need it. This is not to say that many people enjoy a great college experience of liberal arts and feel that gives them a good all-around background for whatever else they plan to study.

College is good,* but so are the many other potential pathways to educational and work success.

I guess I'm not supposed to remind you that Steve Jobs, Bill Gates, and Michael Dell (Apple, Microsoft, Dell Computers) all, uh, "dropped out" of college...and look what happened to them!

You know who you are. You know what you want. Don't spend your scholarship money foolishly, or squander your parents' money, or go into long-term debt until you are sure that what you're buying is what you want and need.

**No, I didn't go to college, but I took lots of classes, and have read at least 1,000 books, and just might go to "real college" after I retire!*

Job Title: Certified Public Accountant

Success

Don't come looking for me on the weekends—I'll be gone fishing. Nothing beats cranking up my twin Evinrude engines and heading off deep-sea fishing. Because I'm a Certified Public Accountant (CPA), I can afford to play hard. Some people live to work, but my crew and I work to live, and play. When I started off, I worked for a company doing tax accounting and account audits, but now I work for myself. I built a base of steady clients and I add new ones wherever I go—I'm turning down work because I can't handle it all. Don't get me wrong, I love my job, but financial stability and living my life how I want makes going to work a pleasure.

Taxes, Taxes, Taxes

Most people I know dread doing their taxes. Let's face it: finances are just a messy affair, so my job is to untangle all the threads. My biggest clients are companies that need their finances managed, tax accounts audited, or budgets planned. Everybody pays taxes, so it's logical that the number of CPA jobs is increasing at an average rate.

Skills

Most of my job is performed on special accounting software, but that doesn't mean my math skills are shoddy, and I can use several accounting systems. I take pride in being personable and professional—I can talk to anyone, anytime, and it's my job to convince businesses that their financial lives are in good hands.

Education

A Bachelor's degree in Accounting is required before you can take the CPA certification exam. Some states have additional requirements as well, so check those out beforehand. Why did I choose to be a CPA? Well, I had my heart set on being a veterinarian, but school really hit me hard. I gave up, until my uncle suggested I look into public accounting. I did a complete 180-degree turnaround in my education and couldn't be happier. I will warn you though; the certification exam is no joke. They say life is a test, but for a while, studying for that test was my life!

Financial Factor

If you work for a small company, the highest salaries are usually found in bookkeeping and payroll. CPAs make anywhere from $45,000–$78,000/year, but my salary directly depends on how much work I want to put in. Since I own my own accounting practice, I'm responsible for independent contracting, setting fees, and managing my workload.

If I Could Go Back

I watch too much of the Discovery Channel's *The Deadliest Catch.* I have this dream of being an Alaskan fisherman, but I don't think I'd trade my job security. Besides, I have a family that would miss me.

Shortcut to Success

If you have a clue as to what you'd like to do, then a good bet is to learn about that kind of work NOW, and what it is expected to be like in the future.

One of the main complaints of hiring managers is that "kids" don't have the skills required for the jobs they have to fill (and often not a strong enough education to make it worth training you). Ouch!

A Master's degree in Pop Culture sounds like a great idea, until you look for a job. One day you can be anything you want to be, even if you have to start your own company to do it. In the meantime, this is the real world and employers are looking for real skills.

One disturbing trend is that if you take courses at a poor quality educational institution, and they train you for "yesterday" (on old technology or tools, and outdated software, for example), then the skills that you paid for and worked hard to earn are virtually worthless in the marketplace.

What do employers do when they can't find adequately skilled talent? "We hire offshore," most say. That means that someone from India, or Iceland, or Venezuela got YOUR job.

Think about it.

Job Title: Cupcake Entrepreneur

Success

Creative baking is my specialty. I have an arsenal of ingredients, and I'm always ready to add more! Combining my art skills with tantalizing flavors and textures to create beautiful and scrumptious cupcakes is what I love about my job! I can do other things like wedding cakes, but how boring is that? I prefer the artistic liberty of being a cupcake entrepreneur.

Small Beginnings

Big things have small beginnings. Growing up in a small community, I wanted to get out in the wider world and make something of myself. I had a lot of people in my life who didn't think I could succeed, but that's what I did. And look, I've turned something as small as a cupcake into a moneymaking business.

Skills

Good basic math skills, cleanliness, and being an excellent communicator are essential! It helps to be artistic, creative, and a little adventurous; otherwise, cupcakes are just sweet bread. I also pride myself in knowing the difference between taste and flavor. What that really means is, you have to know that the details matter!

Education

I've always been artistic, so I went to art school after I earned my high school diploma. Guess what? I flunked out. It wasn't the right fit for me. I went to work at a grocery store in their bakery. Turns out, I really liked decorating the cakes—probably too much. I wanted to put my own touch on them, and that didn't turn out too well, either. That's when I went to work for a specialty bakery in my small town. The owner encouraged me to take some culinary arts classes at a technical school. It really helped! What I learned enhanced my natural talents, and now I've opened my own cupcake bakery called, "Hola, Cupcake!"

Financial Factor

It's better than being a starving artist, that's for sure! When I started out, I was making a little over $20,000/year. No, that's not a lot, but I make a bit more now that I have my own bakery. Just remember, owning a business is no cakewalk, personally or financially.

If I Could Go Back

I would have looked into those classes at the technical school a lot sooner than I did, like right after I flunked out of art school. I would be more honest with myself about my abilities, and what I really enjoy doing. It's no coincidence that I wanted to work in the bakery at the grocery store! I've always loved baking. It just took me a while to figure out that being a creative baker can be a fabulous career!

Marketable Skills

A great thing to bring to the job interview table is as many "marketable skills" as you can obtain.

Once upon a time, skills such as carpentry, typography, typing, stenography, welding, ironworking, and many others virtually meant an instant job because those skills were in big demand. But times change (often by the hour!), so keep up with the times.

Once a degree in humanities was a fine choice (and for some folks, still is), but today far more jobs are available for people with degrees in applied sciences such as food biology, microbiology, and entomology. You can't be lazy; you have to learn the choices, what's rapidly becoming outmoded and undesired, and what's coming up on the radar screen for jobs, just when you want one.

Technology is a general term; *which* technology skills do you intend to get skilled in? By the time we hire folks for jobs that you recognize the names of, we are already preparing to hire people with jobs we don't know the names of yet, but we know we will need those skills.

Sound confusing? Sound hard? Work is work. Getting a job is work. But nailing emerging skills is a real competitive asset. Take a look at the names of the jobs in this book. They were not necessarily called the same thing in the past, and soon they may have a new name (and new skill requirements) as the work world and technology march on.

It's a moving target, I know. But you like games, remember?!

Job Title: Computer Application Software Engineer

Success

I own a small application (app) development company—pretty smart, huh? Our apps are changing the way you access information, play games, and connect with your friends—this isn't a fad, apps are here to stay. Like most start-up businesses, we don't have a set daily routine. Like today, I spent the morning working on code for an app update and did some accounting. In the afternoon, I visited a client for a proposal, researched a new technology tool, and released a press statement. I'll leave you with this bad joke: The key to life fulfillment is finding a job that brings you app-iness.

Education

I didn't learn all the tricks on my own. Parts I figured out because I liked computers, but curiosity only got me so far. I needed education and training. Employers require a Bachelor's degree in Computer Science or Software Engineering. Application developers don't always write code, but you need to learn the basics of computer programming in school. I consider myself a polyglot—I can't speak Chinese or Spanish, but I use computer languages like Java for Android, HTML for web development, and Ruby for scripting. Technology is moving so fast, you'll be learning new tools all your life. I hope you like the fast-paced world.

App-ly Yourself

Not all computer application software engineers are app developers. In fact, most work for companies developing underlying computer software networks. They create safe and closed application codes, more efficient systems and user-friendly interfaces for office and home software. This job is in high demand and you really could work anywhere.

Financial Factor

$90,000/year isn't too shabby for a tech geek. I started off with a lot less than that, working part time for a web-content software developer, but starting my own business was the right idea. Now as a business owner, I could cut myself more of the profits, but I'd rather invest money in new technology and training for our employees.

Skills

Serious technical skills are needed as well as good communication and analytical skills. Application software development is a team effort that sees the project through from beginning to end, so I hope you play well with others. Also, keep in mind, it's an innovative, problem-solving job; new apps can be outdated or become useless.

If I Could Go Back

With the software skills I have now, I would like to be a video-game programmer, but it's not often that I wish I'd taken another route. Sometimes the programs get tedious and methodically mind-numbing, but a big bag of Doritos and Mountain Dew gets me through.

A is for Ambiguity

ambiguity [am-buh-gyoo-eh-tee] **doubtful, uncertain, changing; open to more than one interpretation**

The number one complaint employers have about employees is their inability to understand or handle ambiguity.

If something is ambiguous, it's often difficult to deal with because the answers are not clear; really, the questions are not necessarily clear. Even in the process of "figuring it out," facts, questions, answers, circumstances, and many other variables vary, wobble, wiggle, turn inside out, and everything else they can do to confuse and confound the issue.

We have plenty of ambiguity in our daily lives: which outfit to wear; did our teacher mean this or did she really mean that?; so am I getting the scholarship/job/etc., or not—I got such mixed signals?; and how will I solve the problem of being in two places at once, 'cause I need to be?

In the work world, ambiguous circumstances are constant. That's why we call it work. That's why there are "problems" to solve. Blank paper on which YOU are expected to write, invent, create, solve, explain, flowchart.

On a work team, new facts, changed facts (now that's ambiguity!), differing opinions, new directives from the boss, altered circumstances—all these lead to the necessity of keeping an open mind, paying attention, keeping up with the details, and a willingness and ability to continue to move forward in "working it all out," or suggesting a drastic change, or even an end to the project.

It's almost impossible to explain ambiguity, especially in the swiftly moving river of day-to-day workflow, where things move fast, change often, and you are expected to keep up. Some of us find that fun. Learn to be a person who can do more than go with the flow, but who is always ready and willing to nod with understanding and then be enthusiastic and positive about moving in the new direction, no matter how often that happens—often very often!

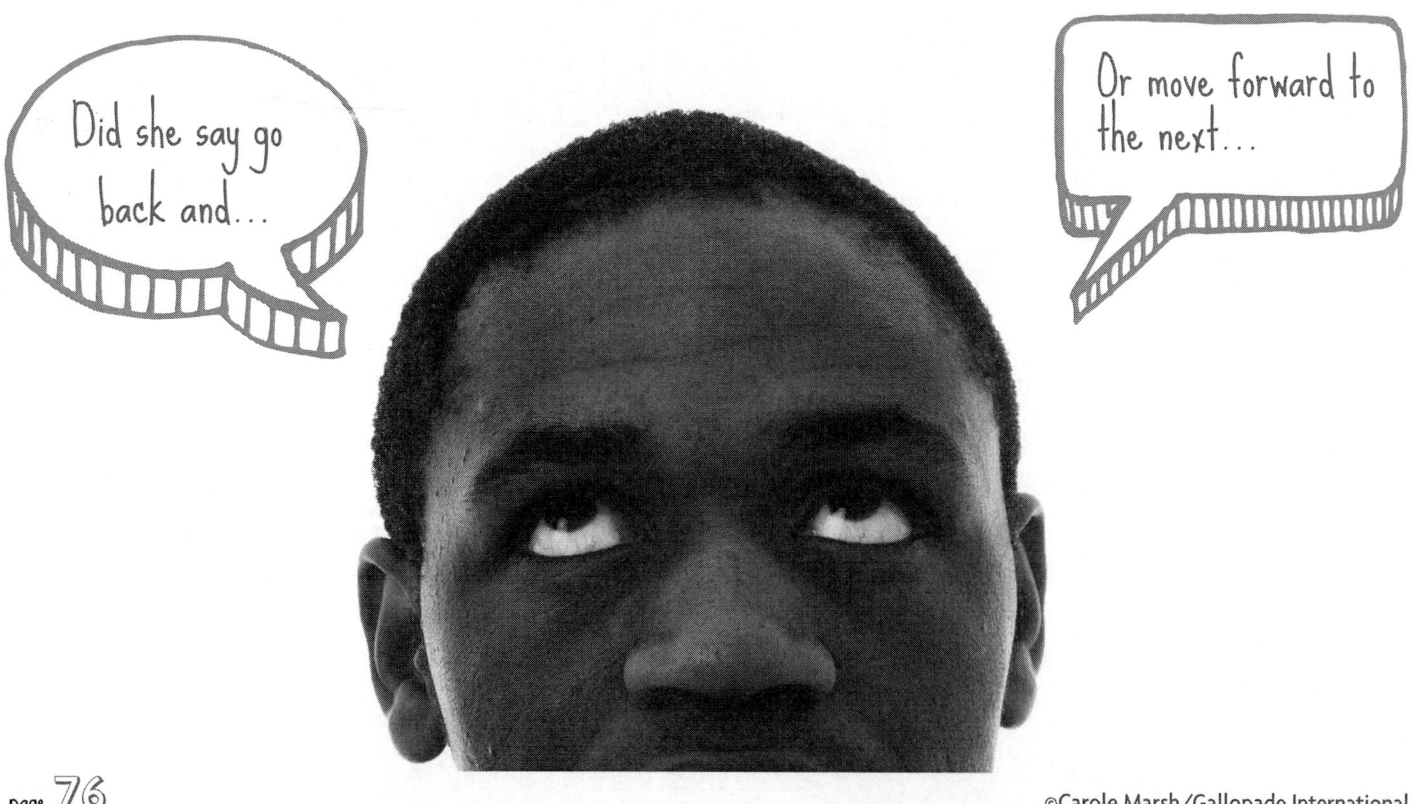

Job Title: Boilermaker

Success

This job explains itself, really—boilermakers make boilers. Simple, right? The trick is learning the specialized tools and the skills for installing boilers. What I'm saying is, a surgeon or tax accountant can't do my job because he/she won't know squat about how a boiler works—nor how to weld, install, and maintain the boiler instruments in factories and breweries. I take pride in the work I do, mainly because it's active and challenging—I'm always thinking on my feet. It's great to work full-time (unlike most other construction jobs, which work on contract), make good money, and have a blast meeting new people.

Underwater Welding

This is an associated career, like welding, brazing, and pipefitting. If you can scuba dive and weld at the same time, jobs are waiting for you on America's coastlines. I have friends who are commercial divers and are trained in underwater welding (or wet-welding) techniques; they work on securing underwater structures, repairing old tankers, and maintaining oilrigs. Think you can handle the pressure?

Skills

I'm a strong person—physically and mentally. I can do tiring work for long hours, like moving large vat pieces without getting fatigued or losing mental focus. Sometimes I have to work in tight and high spaces, so being afraid of heights or getting claustrophobic is a sign that your boilermaker career is going to burst.

Education

I started off, like most boilermakers do—as a welder. I took welding classes in high school, graduated, and lived with my parents (no shame in that!) until I had my TIG and MIG certifications. Then I did contract jobs for a while, but the work wasn't steady. The path to being a boilermaker requires an apprenticeship of some kind, usually four to five years of paid, on-the-job training. I had the luxury of already being a certified welder, which really stuck two and two together. There are several apprenticeship programs available, and one offered by The International Brotherhood of Boilers, but be careful where you go for education. You want skills certified, so do your research first!

Financial Factor

Being a standard welder will pay the bills—I earned about $29,000. Like I said, a welder's work is inconsistent, so I transferred my welding skills to becoming a boilermaker, and now I'm earning about $50,000/year. Anyone can tell you that's the difference between getting by and living comfortably.

If I Could Go Back

I didn't realize the value of experience—ANY experience, especially work-related experience in high school or college. Although I took welding classes in my high school's vocational programs and got welding certifications, landing jobs was almost impossible because I had no work experience... none, zilch.

It's All in the Manual

When you get your first job (after the lemonade stand, grass-cutting, paper route, babysitting—all great experiences), read the Employee Manual. In fact, learn everything you can about all the new things, such as W2 forms, payroll deductions, and everything else, because you will see these things all your work life, and it just makes sense to learn what they mean.

The Employee Manual means you. I was amused (and saddened) when a friend told me that Delta Airlines had felt compelled to send out a "How to be absent from work" letter to all employees, since, it appears, they did not seem to grasp the courtesies/requirements of letting their supervisor know when they would be out, for sudden illness, for example. The Employee Manual tells you such things. There may also be fine print that says what the repercussions are for infractions of the rules. This is not school. There are rules and there are consequences, including "immediate dismissal." It pays to know the rules.

Read any update memos or e-mails, too. You just might want to know what the rules are on Internet usage at work, or, for example, if your phone calls or computer usage are monitored. There are rules, and there are even laws. Some things may even be benefits to you that you won't know to ask about if you don't read the manual.

It's best not to assume that it's OK to use your cell phone at will at work, or to surf the Internet, or to text outside the company, or inside, as far as that goes.

Once you know the rules, obey them. A lot of thought went into such rules and regulations to make your workplace a better place. You might not like or agree with all the rules, but one day, you may be the supervisor charged with ensuring that the rules are obeyed. You may even write the next Employee Manual!

These rules are not requests, by the way. Business means business.

Job Title: Nurse Anesthetist

Success

Anesthesia refers to the loss of sensation induced by pain-blocking drugs used in medical procedures. Have you ever been put to sleep—I mean, medically? As a Certified Registered Nurse Anesthetist (CRNA), I'm the last person you'll see before an operation and the first person you'll see when waking up. I have a lot of responsibilities, mostly related to keeping you alive and pain-free during a procedure; therefore, I'm treated with a lot of respect in the medical field. I worked in the ER for a while, always on call, and loved it, but I have a child and needed more steady working hours. Now I'm employed by a plastic surgeon. The pay is great and I can afford to give my daughter a comfortable life. I do the things I want, too—just last month, I took a medical vacation to Brazil to assist charity medical teams in poor shantytowns.

Career Options

A great thing about a career in anesthesia is versatility. Most anesthesia providers work in hospitals, but a certified nurse anesthetist can work anywhere anesthesia is provided, including delivery rooms or the offices of dentists, ophthalmologists, podiatrists, and pain management specialists.

Skills

Patience and a detail-oriented personality are essentials. The anesthesia field requires social skills—the medical field is a team environment and you need to understand that many doctors and medical professionals can have grossly bloated egos. I've learned to deal with temperamental types. You should also have good hand-eye coordination and the ability to stay calm under extreme, life-or-death circumstances.

Education

As one of the most advanced nursing careers, this job requires lots of training and education. Believe it or not, I got my start in the military, where I got medical training and practical experience. The military helped pay for my Bachelor of Science degree in Nursing (BNS). After nursing certification, I applied to an anesthesia program and graduated third in my class. You know, the funny thing is I almost failed chemistry in undergraduate—that teacher hated me, I think.

Financial Factor

The medical world is very good to me. I make around $110,000/year, and that's because I don't take late night call or work separate contracts—I could make a lot more! The average salary for nurse anesthetists is $130,000/year. Not too bad, huh?

If I Could Go Back

There's no going back, so why would I? All of the mistakes I made along the way have made me who I am. I had a kid earlier than my finances could handle, and I wasn't always around because of being in the military, but I think we're a strong family now, and I have a great job to support the ones I love.

Why Writing...

...is such an important essential 21st century skill

Can you...

- Write a compelling argument of why you are suited to lead a task team project?
- Support your claim of why you need a budget of X dollars to spend on new tools, equipment, or a research trip to Hawaii?
- Write an analysis of gathered information for a go/no go decision?
- Build a list of relevant data to justify why you did something a certain way?
- Write a "how to" document, guide, or program to explain to a novice how to clearly perform a task?
- Convey complex ideas or concepts with brevity, clarity, and impact.
- Use specifics, details, or story-telling narratives to convince someone of your point of view?

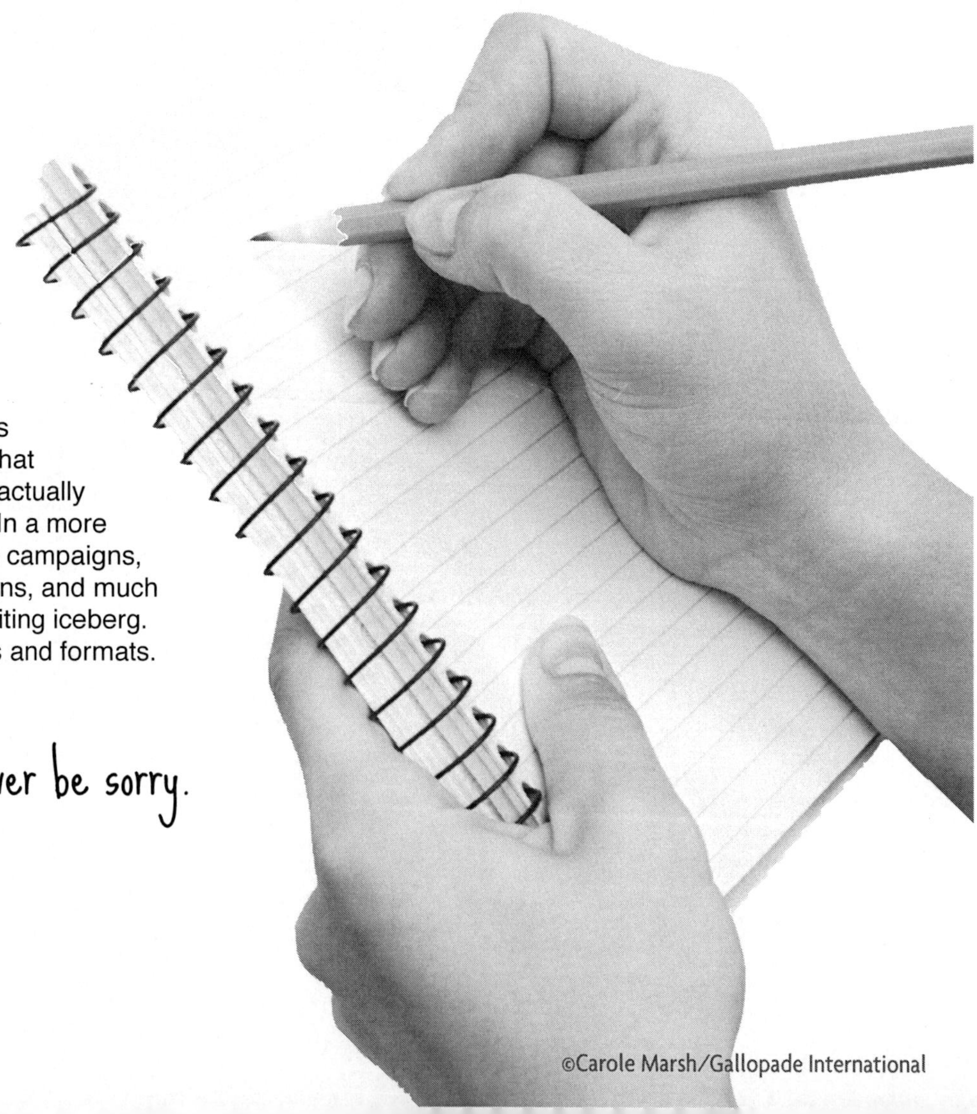

These are just a very, very few examples of ordinary day-to-day business writing that you may not only be required to do, but actually want to do—and enjoy, not suffer over. In a more creative, marketing vein, there are sales campaigns, sales call sheets, ads, publicity campaigns, and much more. Again, this is just the tip of the writing iceberg. Don't forget writing for digital documents and formats.

Learn to write well; you'll never be sorry.

Job Title: Aerial Photographer

Success

Have you ever wanted to see the unknown places of the world? Or, from a helicopter, photograph the London sprawl lit up at dusk? I just wanted to travel. I've specialized in aerial photography since 2003, worked with clients like Coca-Cola, BP, and Nike, and got paid to travel! No worries, I still find time to take the pictures I want, but I love the challenge of meeting deadlines, marketing myself, and getting that perfect cover shot—take it from me, it's not as easy as point and shoot.

My Tech

I carry my two babies at all times: my trusty Nikon D700 and a newer Nikon D3X, both digital single lens reflex (DSLR). I love everything Nikon, Adobe, and Apple! Yeah, I'm a tech snob, but it's not about being flashy. It's about having options—the perfect combination of filters, color balance and stability control. I'm not picky; I'm a perfectionist!

Skills

Artistic ability should be your motivation, the reason you pursue photography. But there are plenty of unknown Ansel Adamses—to really pop out from the competition, you need business skills, knowing how to give clients what they want. Also, you'll need to know various computer programs used for postproduction and photo editing.

Education

I never went to college. Straight out of high school, I worked retail and learned a thing or two about making customers happy. As a child, I played around with those disposable Kodak cameras and then a little instant Polaroid. I used a portfolio from my high school black and white photography class to land a wedding photography apprenticeship. I was looking for new ways to get photographs and expand my portfolio, so I went out to the local airport and asked to fly with some of the pilots. After that first flight, I knew what my life was going to be about—I was breathless. My training was all on-the-job, and I'm still learning. If you're interested in science photography or a photojournalism career, a college degree is required. Even if you're a sharpshooter, don't shrug off education. Training and practice make expertise.

Financial Factor

The quickest way to make money at photography is to sell your camera—but not the best way by far. The average photographer makes $30,000/year, but between my collection of stock photos available online, commissioned work for big companies, and photo book collections, I made about $65,000 last year, not to mention paid travel time!

If I Could Go Back

My first-year finances were like a monster living in my studio closet. I didn't want to see them or acknowledge their existence. Business and accounting classes would have made my life easier.

The Global Achievement Gap

Author Tony Wagner has created a list of the "Seven Survival Skills of the 21st Century." You can agree or disagree, but...well, he's an expert. The comments in italics are mine.

1. **Critical thinking and problem solving:** *Jobs are not school; there is neither time, budget, nor the desire to teach you things you should have already learned.*
2. **Collaboration across networks and leading by influence:** *Work is done in teams, often miles or nations apart; you must be able to communicate, reason, and persuade.*
3. **Agility and adaptability:** *You must be able to learn on the fly, change rapidly, adapt, and adroitly use methods and tools that you didn't expect to use.*
4. **Initiative and Entrepreneurism:** *Are you self-directed, a creative problem-solver, quick on your mental feet, willing to speak up, and able to lead by example?*
5. **Effective Oral and Written Communication:** *Can you express yourself in a brief, clear manner?*
6. **Accessing and Analyzing Information:** *Can you handle the onslaught of data that will come your way and determine which is important?*
7. **Curiosity and Imagination:** *Work is not a "sit on the sidelines" sport; you must be able to think, challenge, inquire, decide, and act.*

I could tell you what to do about all this, but that would defeat the purpose—you figure it out this time! Pretend that... it's your job!

Job Title: Systems Network Engineer

Success

I'm responsible for the "plumbing" of a company's computers. Just like hitting a water pipe with a hammer isn't a fix-all, resetting the router doesn't always fix your Wi-Fi. Did you know that the Internet, and intranets, have multiple levels in their digital structures? The technical classification of my job is a high-level technical analyst specializing in local area networks (LAN) and wide area networks (WAN), but it's really not that complicated. My job is to design, set up and maintain the communication systems for businesses. In the IT world, being a network engineer is one of the best-paid jobs around—I'm making ends meet working for the information giant known as Google.

Education

Network engineers need lots of technical training, requiring a Bachelor's degree in Network Management, Computer Engineering, or Information Science. A degree will get your foot in the door but most of the training is on the job, and there are several specific certifications available (for example, Cisco Systems certification). Yeah, math, computer science, and engineering classes in undergraduate will help you out, but routing and networking is a mindset—understanding how stuff flows from one place to another. Do you have the willpower to sit in front of a problem at 3 a.m. when all your systems bite the dust and there's nobody else around to fix it? Don't worry, you can ease your way into the job with internships and entry-level starting positions.

Stay Connected

It's an exciting time to be a network engineer—new tools like cloud computing, mobile sharing, and high-speed social networks are making it easier to stay connected with anyone anywhere. Businesses everywhere need faster, more reliable information systems that require network engineers. It's one of the FASTEST growing career fields, and it's no wonder why.

Financial Factor

My average salary for the last five years has been $65,000, but the range is anywhere from $40,000 to $100,000/year depending on who you work for, what certifications you have, and how much experience you gain. After several years' experience, you might move up to a senior network engineering position.

Skills

Would you ever guess you might need computer skills? Really, it's a "noodly" job—you have to think your way through jobs and understand how stuff works—you know, analytical skills. It also helps to develop a detailed understanding of electronics and mechanical workings.

If I Could Go Back

My senior manager started off with nothing but a degree in literature and a lot of enthusiasm. I wish that things were that simple still, and that I could have explored more liberal arts courses in college.

My Little Tin Box

For a long time, when I was just starting out in the business world, I kept a small metal box filled with inspirational quotations. When I was stumped or just needed a kind word or two, I'd open the box and read them. It surprised me how often I repeated these phrases of advice to myself when I was making a tough decision or facing a challenge. I guess this was a way to mentor myself with wise voices, often from the past. Create your own box, envelope, or screensaver advice wall. Here are a few of my "faves," old and new; you're welcome to copy this page, snip them out and use them to get started.

Yesterday's solutions don't solve tomorrow's problems.

Don't look back unless you want to go that way.

"Being a [woman], what more could you want to be?"—Eleanor Roosevelt [Substitute any word you wish.]

Don't reign your horse in…just when it is about to jump.

A failure just proves that something won't work that way…at this time.

"Don't you want to make a dent in the future?"—Steve Jobs

Don't have a job, have a passion.

Take the course opposite to custom…you'll almost always do well.

So what if you are misunderstood? So were Jesus, Galileo, Pythagoras, and every other wise and great person.

Try, try again.

Never give up. Never give up. Never give up.

Make mistakes.

Create your own sense of beautiful.

Rewrite the rules.

"Get good at doing the impossible; that's what most people want, need, and pay well for."—Carole Marsh (Hey, it's my book!)

Enjoy the ride.

"Purple's always nice."

Job Title: Organizer

Success

Not to sound like your mom, but I really do believe there is a place for everything and everything should be in its place! It makes things so much simpler. The cool thing for me is that I can look at someone's messy desk or disorganized office or cluttered cabinets, and I can see exactly how it all needs to be. Not everyone can figure out how to organize their stuff, and a lot of people really need someone to help them do just that (or to do it for them). That's where a home or work organizer comes in!

Cool Tools

I mostly use my brain, but I also have an iPad and a MacBook Pro. I use computer-aided design (CAD) software, too. Some great software is available for digital organization of documents and accounting info. I don't use those myself; I just recommend them!

Skills

An eye for detail, good problem-solving skills, and a flair for neatness and efficiency are all required! Having good people skills and patience helps in most jobs—especially this one.

Education

A college degree isn't necessary. I started out working as a file clerk for a marketing firm. My job required me to file paperwork in many different offices. It wasn't long before I came up with a streamlined and better, faster filing system. Plus, I didn't even realize I was doing this, but I often reorganized other areas of the office—the storage closet, the break room, places like that—I just thought I was "straightening up" the mess! After a while, I realized I had a knack for making the most of any space. The rest, as they say, is history!

Financial Factor

At first, I did all my professional organizing in my free time while I was a file clerk. Once I realized it could be an actual job, I went to work for a redesign company, and I started out making about the same salary as I had been making, but doing the work I loved. Eventually, I decided to go to work for myself, and now I've more than doubled my salary. My fees vary depending on the actual job, but I make between $39 and $100 an hour now!

If I Could Go Back

It was actually not too bad getting where I am, but there were a couple of bumps in the road. I was fired from my first job right out of high school. Want to know why? My boss went on vacation, and I organized her desk. She came back and said she couldn't find anything and was so mad she fired me on the spot! I would've taken classes on CAD instead of teaching myself. It took that way, and I could have avoided lot of trial and error.

What Did You Fail At Today?

Be willing to try. Be willing to fail. Einstein, Edison, all those brilliant guys whose names start with E were good at failure. You can't succeed if you won't allow yourself to fail. Failure is how you learn. Often the bigger the failure, the greater the gained knowledge (and never forgotten, which is an asset in itself).

Here are just a few things I've failed at (using my own personal definition of failure, which is probably harsher than others would judge me; you'll likely be the same way...don't be so hard on yourself. Dust off, get up, get back on the horse)!

Being born; I was three months premature.
My eye test—over and over and over.
Most math.
Spelling; I'm a horrible speller, but that's what dictionaries are for.
Everything I've ever written the first time; that's why they call them first drafts.
Chemistry and other assorted scientific subjects.
Anything related to motors and such.
Sewing—boy, was I bad at that!
Accounting: I invented accounting. (Really! I didn't know someone else already had!) I'm great at inventory but a failure at counting.
Management: I like for everyone to do what they want to do—not a good recipe for managing.
Meetings: I tend to fall asleep.
Remembering faces, but I never forget an idea.
Swimming, skiing, softball, soccer, bowling, chess, well you get the picture: sports, all of 'em.
Parallel parking: ain't gonna happen; ain't ever gonna ace that one.
Mixing plastic, grass, and chocolate chips and trying to mail them to impress my customers...it's a long story and a sad, embarrassing one at that.
Lots of other stuff.

Nonetheless, I'm an absolute success, highly-skilled, in big demand, having fun, changing lives, and making lots of money.

I do believe there's a lesson in all this for you, but I do not have time to explain—I have some failing to do. What will you fail at today? Failure is ALWAYS an option—go for it!

Job Title: Personal Stylist and Shopper

Success

I live for fashion and love keeping up with the latest styles and trends! With my job, research is reading a fashion magazine, going to fashion shows, and shopping at all the hottest stores! I shop for and design looks for everyone from attorneys to television stars. I can create styles that are funky, fashionable, edgy, or traditional depending on the person, place, and purpose for each look.

Cool Tools

I subscribe to every fashion magazine you can think of, and I actually read them! I watch fashion television—all those shows on TV about fashion and design, and I go to as many fashion shows as I possibly can. In other words, if it's about fashion, I read it, watch it, and learn all about it! I also have books to help me with colors and body types.

Skills

Having a flair for fashion and loving to shop are a must! I have a great sense of style, too. I work hard to learn what my clients like (and don't like!). I use my knowledge of colors and body types to help my clients look fabulous in a style that is all their own!

Education

A college degree in fashion helps, but I had to go to work right after high school. While I worked in a trendy, high-fashion clothing store, I read books on fashion and design and learned all I could about top designers, what colors look best together, and what styles are ideal for each body type. I put that knowledge into action with my clients, my family, and my friends, and soon discovered I loved what I was doing and that I was good at it, too. Before long, people were asking for my help, and I had a small business as a personal stylist. My business is still growing, and I'm still learning! I'm taking classes in fashion at a local college to build upon my knowledge, learn more about the industry, and make some professional connections.

Financial Factor

It all depends on you! If you're self-employed (like me!) the sky is really the limit. I've charged clients anywhere from twenty dollars to thousands of dollars for my services. After I got started, I worked for a major retail store, and I made good money there, too. The average salary is around $60,000 a year, but, just remember, that all depends on who you work for, what city you're in, how much experience you have, and your number of clients.

If I Could Go Back

I would have started seriously studying fashion a lot sooner than I did. Trends come and go, it's true, but so many styles go "out" and come back "in" and some styles are simply timeless! I've had a lot of catching up to do, and if I'd started studying styles, body types, colors, designers, fabrics, and all that stuff earlier, it would have been a lot easier, and, who knows, maybe I could have built my business even faster!

Emotional Skills

These don't really show up so much in today's hard-nosed list of essential 21st century skills. They are very important. You don't have to have or acquire them all, but it's only fair that you be made aware of them.

Honesty

Integrity

A sense of fairness

A positive attitude

Being helpful

Politeness

Being open

Not whining

Not complaining

Sharing

Really caring

Being a good listener

Thoughtful

Passionate

Cooperative

A cup half-full, not half-empty kind of person

Generous

Kind

Humble

Sincere

Genuine

Tolerant

Authentic

Bold

Noble

A good leader

A great follower

Responsible

Loyal

There are a lot more, but this list, what does it mean? Well, if you possess or acquire even half these attributes, then you're a responsible adult.

People hire responsible adults.

Job Title: School Counselor

Success

Helping students achieve personally, academically, and socially is my passion. I love that I don't just sit behind a desk all day and that no two days are ever the same. Knowing that I am making a positive impact in my school by helping to identify and resolve problems with individuals and groups, and by finding ways to improve our programs, is inspiring and rewarding!

Cool Tools

Can you believe I get to use social media as part of my job?! Pretty neat, huh? A computer or laptop is essential to my job for research, recordkeeping, and testing. Believe it or not, another valuable tool is relationships—with my co-workers, with parents, with other counseling professionals, and, most of all, with my students.

Skills

Do you listen more than you talk? Can you communicate effectively and efficiently (without lecturing or using too many words)? If so, you're on the right path! I've always loved working with kids and teenagers, and I especially like helping and encouraging them. It's essential that I am a team player—I work with everyone in the school including teachers, administrators, students, parents, and other counselors. We all work together for the good of our students and school.

Education

A Master's degree is required to do my job. First, you must earn a Bachelor's degree. This could be in just about any field: education, criminal justice, psychology, communication, English, math, you get the idea! My degree is in Middle Grades Education. While I was teaching middle school language arts and social studies, I attended a pretty big university and earned my Master's in Education in School Counseling. As part of my training, I completed a 100-hour practicum and a 600-hour internship.

Financial Factor

School counselors usually work for public or private schools, so their pay varies depending on the school system and years of experience. The average pay for school counselors is around $50,000 a year. My experience teaching middle school before I became a counselor has increased my salary.

If I Could Go Back

I don't think I ever met my school counselor. I would have stopped in and said hey! I thought counselors were for people with big problems. That's just not true. Everybody needs help sometimes, or at least some good advice. Come see me!

Before I Was, I Was...

Once I wrote a poem...

> **Before I Was, I Was...**
>
> **Sunbeam flakes**
> **Teddy bear fuzz**
> **Moonlight licks**
> **Rainbow stripes**
> **Etc.**

Sort of silly, but true.

Before you are YOU, the SUCCESS, you may very well be something else, perhaps many things, and each will accrue to your eventual success, so do not underestimate these stepping stones. After all, they may help you see what you don't really want to be, or lead to what you really want to do. No work is ever wasted. No experience comes without benefits. Use them all to build skills, contacts, confidence, and business and people savviness.

BEFORE...

Walt Disney created Mickey Mouse...he was an ambulance driver

Alfred Hitchcock made spine-tingling thrillers...he made simple title cards

Merv Griffin started a game show revolution...he was a church organist

Madeleine Albright was U.S. Secretary of State...she sold bras in a department store

Jennifer Aniston became a movie star...she was a waitress

Sean Connery became James Bond...he polished coffins

Johnny Depp became a pirate...he was a telemarketer

Sheryl Crow became a music star...she was an elementary school teacher

Jon Bon Jovi made Christmas decorations; Tom Cruise was a paperboy; Clay Aiken was a YMCA counselor; Lady Gaga was a waitress; David Letterman was a stock boy; Harrison Ford was a carpenter; Michael Dell was a dishwasher; Ashanti worked in daycare...and on and on!

WHAT WILL YOU BE BEFORE?

Job Title: Solar Energy Tech

Success

I'm sure you've heard people talking—parents complaining about electricity bills and everybody moaning about gas prices. Renewable energy sources like solar, wind, and hydrogen power are hot topics in the job market. As a solar energy technician, I install, maintain, and monitor photovoltaic systems—in simple terms, I know everything about solar panels. I'm not a hippie or a bleeding heart with grand visions of world peace, but I do believe in practical solutions. I work for a major electric company helping large businesses that are looking to cut costs and go green. After installation, I have long-term job security maintaining and updating the solar technology.

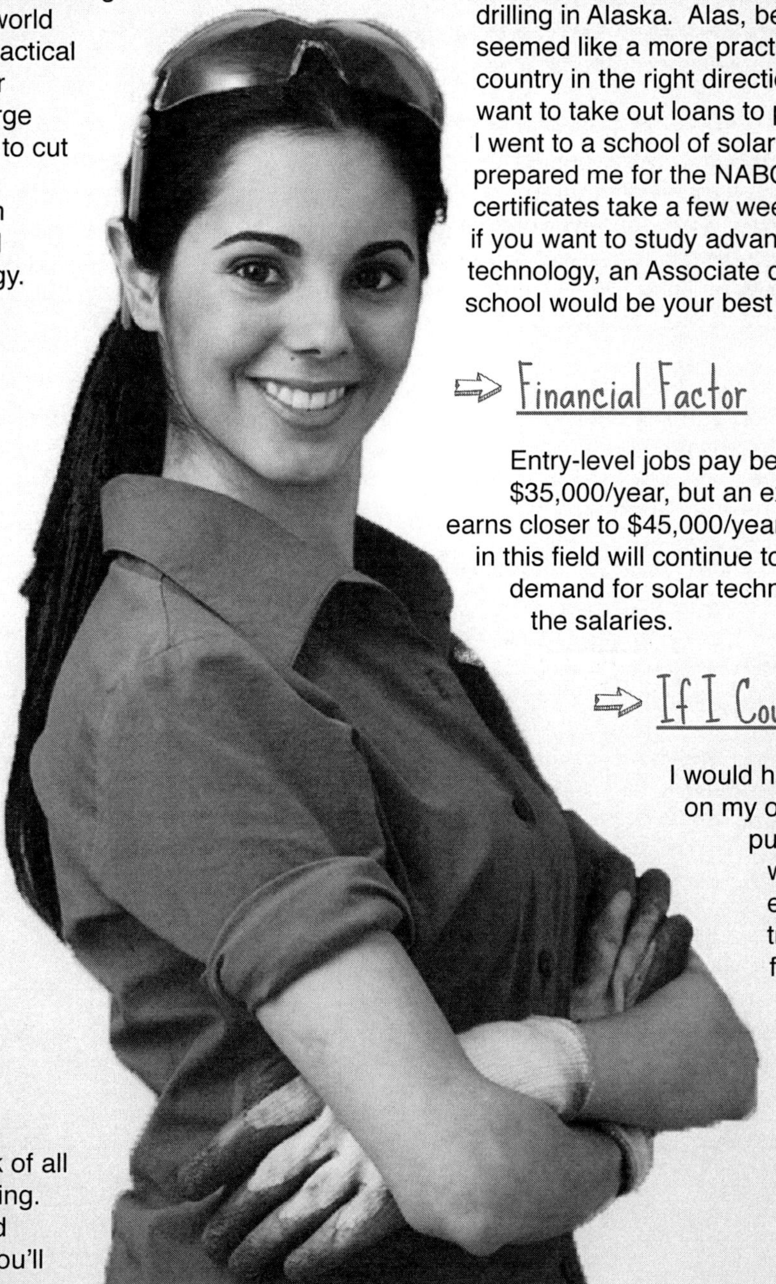

Power the Future

My thoughts are that coal, oil, and natural gas are great, for now, but solar power, wind power, and hydrogen fuel are real solutions to the world's energy woes. Renewable energy jobs, including solar energy, are expected to be a hot commodity. Seriously, the sun is shining on this career—some estimates say that by 2030, one-in-four jobs will relate to renewable energy!

Skills

Being adaptable is the most important thing. Like a "jack of all trades," I'm constantly learning. You need to be mentally and physically sharp, because you'll be reading blueprints, solving complex problems on the fly, and performing technical tasks like modifications and physical installation.

Education

I always liked the idea of an energy-related career—my parents pleaded with me to be a geologist in the oil industry. I told them I think the oil businesses are evil and that I wanted to lobby against the oil drilling in Alaska. Alas, being a solar energy tech seemed like a more practical way to move our country in the right direction. Besides, I didn't want to take out loans to pay for college. Instead I went to a school of solar technology, which also prepared me for the NABCEP exams. Some certificates take a few weeks to a year to earn, or if you want to study advancing renewable energy technology, an Associate degree from a technical school would be your best bet.

Financial Factor

Entry-level jobs pay between $25,000 and $35,000/year, but an experienced technician earns closer to $45,000/year. The job prospects in this field will continue to increase, and as the demand for solar technology goes up, so will the salaries.

If I Could Go Back

I would have done more studying on my own. I thought the public school system was responsible for my education, but that's not true. I'm responsible for my education, and I should have studied what interested me sooner. It really would have given me a leg up on the competition.

Specialize

One way to build a good focused skill set, educational path, and job destination is to determine a "specialty" area that you feel would interest you and that you'd love to have as a career. Check out a career pathways website, but then think one to two layers down (and you may have to Google more info) to come up with a specialized type of job.

In business, you can be a generalist, or you can be a specialist. Both are good. If you are a generalist, you can go many directions. If you specialize in something, you may be the ideal job candidate (above all others) for that type of job.

It's one thing to say you are a journalist, but another to say your specialty is investigative journalism…to say you are a cosmetologist vs. you specialize in horror movie prosthetics…to say you are a welder, but your specialty is underwater offshore welding. I almost never have a just-out-of-college grad come to me claiming some specialty. The ones I could use are publishing database management, mailing list demographic targeting, website catalog creation, and such. Think what time it would save me…how that person would stick out from the applicant crowd…and how I might pay a premium for the right candidate with the perfect talents.

I am a writer, but one of my specialties is educational children's mystery genre fiction. You can have more than one specialty. But when you can specify your skills into "I'm job-ready" sound bites, an employer just might take a bite when you're fishing for a job!

Job Title: Recreational Therapist

Success

People ask me if I get depressed working with disabled people. I just shake my head because they obviously don't know anything about what I do. Of course, I get sad seeing a person struggle with severe illness or the loss of body function, but my job is about empowerment. I find what a person needs and then help him or her become active again; I also plan events and track progress. I use sports, games, music, arts, and crafts to help patients build confidence and get back to living life. So, the overwhelming answer is no, I don't get depressed. Seeing empowerment in a patient is what keeps me going and loving my job.

Adventure Therapy

Adventure therapy works on the same idea: people can overcome issues by being active and bold in their lives. Activities can be things like challenge rope-courses, climbing walls, cooperative games, and wilderness excursions. If you have a "can-do" attitude, love physical and outdoor activities, and love seeing people grow with confidence, this might be the job for you.

Skills

You must be at ease working with disabled people—I say that because many people are NOT comfortable, and that's a normal response. I remind myself to always be patient and tactful, and I really strive to be imaginative in adapting a game or activity to patient's specific need. And finally, you'll need some basic physical skills for assisting in games.

Education

A Bachelor's degree in Therapeutic Recreation is generally required for this profession in addition to an exam and certification by the NCTRC. While I can't give you advice on where to go for college, I would suggest that you try the field first. In high school, I volunteered with the Special Olympics. After high school, I thought that I wanted to be a geriatrician (I really like talking to old people), so I volunteered at a nursing home. The recreational therapist there encouraged me to pursue a therapy degree in college and she mentored me along the way. Since then, I've worked at a community center, and then moved to a rehabilitation hospital.

Financial Factor

I'm not stashing wads of cash in my briefcase, but I do make a comfortable living and still do what I love. On average, recreation therapists earn approximately $40,000/year. When I worked at the community center, my salary was lower, and working for the hospital, my salary is higher, so it really depends on what you like to do.

If I Could Go Back

A little known fact about me is that I love playing the violin. I almost attended a music school, but my parents frowned on that. They said I'd never find a job. I know that the options for musicians are limited, but I have several college friends who found their niche in the music world—one of them is actually a music therapist. I wonder if I could have combined my passions?

Go Global

Many states' Departments of Education have launched international workforce development initiatives. This means that your educational pathway to a global job should include:

- foreign languages
- cultural awareness
- certain business skills
- certain technical skills

There ARE jobs out there, including in international business, that go unfilled because of a lack of qualified candidates. (Can you say OPPORTUNITY?!) At the end of this book you'll find a website for more information, but you can help yourself if you:

•Decide if you think a global job interests you.

•Consider what international location appeals to you.

•Think if you bring any advantages to the table already: lived in another country, are from another country, speak a second language.

•Choose which "global one-upmanship" skills you'd like to begin building, then get started.

•Read the want-ads in a major paper or online and see which skills are required for jobs that may interest you.

•Tailor your future educational plans, part-time jobs, internships, and other activities to help you build skills and accomplishments that you can put on your resume.

•Keep your bags packed!

Nothing is more frustrating or heartbreaking to an employer than to have a great job opening, and having to let it remain unfilled for lack of talent. Be the talent!

Job Title: Broadcast Journalist

Success

In only three years of military service, I've visited eleven countries. As a military broadcast journalist, I've been a writer, producer, editor, and star of my own segments while handling news bundles and video productions under threat of high-pressure deadlines. I really love the interaction with people, being able to get out and tell people's stories. Plus, I've gained training, confidence, and worldly experience that I feel only the military could give. It might seem like a lot of responsibilities, but the U.S. military provides training. Don't be afraid to discover what you could become.

Army Achievement

I'm in the Army branch of the Armed Forces, but broadcast journalism in all branches of the U.S. Military provides rewarding careers. For me, my most personal achievement was covering the first democratic elections in Afghanistan on my second tour of duty there. I interviewed men and women who went out to vote and exercise their new freedoms despite threats of Taliban bombing. I was writing history as it happened.

Skills

English, journalism, and speech classes in high school will give you a background of essential skills—can you tell a passion for writing is key? You should also be able to keep detailed and accurate records, write clearly and concisely (no fooling around in the military), and research thoroughly. See, military jobs aren't all brawn and no brains!

Education

I graduated from high school with a scholarship for an Associate degree in Journalism to a small college, but I couldn't afford to finish. I was getting anxious, antsy even, to do something; I mean, actively DO something. So I joined the Army on a delayed-entry program, which allowed me to finish my Associate degree and begin active duty with civilian skills. If you're planning to start this career from scratch, I suggest you visit a recruiter, record an audition tape, and send it to the Defense Information School (DINFOS). I can't stress this enough—plenty of would-be journalists are now jet mechanics. Take the military exam, pass through basic training, and then you'll spend eight weeks at DINFOS in Maryland where you'll receive training in video editing, writing feature and sports copy, and on and on. It's a condensed version of what you'd get in junior and senior year in college—all paid for by the U.S. Government. Not too bad, huh?

Financial Factor

I'm earning about $45,000/year during my service, but the Army gives you so much more in total compensation, including housing, healthcare, and tax advantages. You'll be well taken care of for your valuable services.

If I Could Go Back

Go back? I won't ever leave. I love the sense of community and camaraderie in the military, and I get great benefits for being a public servant.

Secret Words

I am looking at words/terms from the mission statements of elementary schools across the U.S. What does that have to do with you? Some of these words are significant. I think if you'd been privy to them earlier and knew what they really meant for your future, well, you might have studied harder or understood better "why" you had to take those classes. However, it's never too late!

vision: if you don't have a vision of your future, get one now

lifelong learner: plan to be one; you must

capable: pick a few skills to be utterly capable at

responsible: practice being so; it's required

success: this is what you are after and every class can move you closer

mastery: choose at least one skill to master, to be the best at

relevant: prepare for tomorrow, keep your knowledge and skills and contacts current, always

rigorous: life is hard, learn to love the rigorous classes that challenge you; the easy way out leads to nothing

enhanced: enhance what you say you can do with real-world experience through extra-curricular activities, volunteering, internships, part-time jobs, and other well-selected projects

qualified: try to get qualified to do something; these new job certificates are a great, inexpensive idea

leadership: never turn down a chance to be the leader; even if you flop, experiencing leadership before you get to the job is much less painful

collaboration: getting along in school is great preparation for working well on a team at work

essential: what's essential changes, but reading comprehension, good vocabulary, spelling, basic math, and all the other elementary school stuff you learned (I hope!) is absolutely essential and just the first step on the road to economic success—so don't skip any steps while in middle, high, post-high school

Job Title: Branding Expert

Success

This isn't just marketing or advertising—it's the next step and the whole step. Branding isn't about awareness. It's about building a product from the ground up: the philosophy, the look, the entire identity of a "brand" new product. Let me explain: branding is about convincing your users that your product is the only solution to their problem, otherwise they are still shopping. For example, people often say "Kleenex" instead of tissue, because the brand name is so powerful. As a branding expert, I advise companies on how to build a brand identity that firmly establishes their product in the market. My work is always challenging, busy, and extremely rewarding.

Ill-managed Brands

Besides establishing new brands, branding consultants who work for advertising firms help companies maintain their images. With the economic downturn, many companies, once brand-name giants, flopped and bled away their years of good branding. Somewhere along the way, companies like Kmart and Circuit City became irrelevant.

Skills

I use all of my creativity and intellect to get each brand to market—it's incredibly challenging, and incredibly sweet to see your ideas become real world successes. I'm analytical and have honed my business sense to a T. If you're an extroverted people person, that's a great start, but you'll also learn to be dynamic, flexible, and intuitively fluent in the business market.

Education

Entry-level positions in a marketing department or consulting firm usually require a Bachelor's degree in Marketing or Business Administration. I know the idea of school isn't always a pleasant one, but you really have a lot to gain. I didn't just wake up a branding expert—I put in hard work and learned from my mistakes. I learned the tricks of the trade as a brand assistant for an experienced branding consultant—I think that's the best way to go, but other entry-level jobs that can lead to branding are anything relating to sales or management analysis at a consulting firm. Nowadays, more and more branding consultants are going back to school for a Master's degree specifically in Branding.

Financial Factor

It all depends on where you work and the success of your branding. Some brand consultants start at $40,000/year while a senior branding expert can make more than $130,000/year.

If I Could Go Back

I would start my own consulting firm, but I don't have to go back to do that. In fact, I'm better off now that I have lots of experience in the field. I'm planning to start my own firm and use some new ideas that my mentors never dreamed of. Don't ask, because I'm not sharing!

Self-Sufficient

Employers love employees (even new ones) who are self-sufficient. I am your new boss, not your babysitter. I have a job to do, including managing you. There may seem many reasons for you to ask, "Where do I hang my jacket?" "Who's going to set up my computer?" "Can I borrow some paper?" But don't.

I had a college intern this summer and he just cracked me up. He never asked a thing. I asked my assistant, "Has he been working here all this time and I didn't know it?" She just laughed. You could say he was a big boy. He just seemed to set up his own desk, computer, and went right to work. All his questions were reserved for work. Pretty soon, I felt I was working for him—he was sending so much great writing to edit. His questions were few but on target and essential. He was so instantly competent that we left him in charge of the CEO's office while my assistant and I were on vacation. Wow! I loved that guy.

Yes, it takes a certain amount of gumption, experience, common sense *(ahhhh*, comomon sense!), *savoir faire* (look it up), moxie, and an aim to please to pull this off. No, he was not cocky and show-off; he was genuine and authentic, eager and enthusiastic, professional and poised. Yes, it is rare to see this finesse in an intern, or a new, first job, employee.

If your mom still picks up your dirty clothes, if your teachers have to remind you of ANYTHING, if you are always losing things, or forgetting, or depending on others, well NOW would be a good time to grow up and be self-sufficient. Learn to make your own plane reservations, plan an itinerary, do your own spell-checking, write a perfect letter, make a "got results" phone call, and all the other ordinary, self-sufficient things that are really No Big Deal—they are the backdrop of the daily business world that gives you a chance to get down to your real work.

Job Title: Teacher

Success

I love introducing kids to new ideas, information, and technology. I am lucky enough to experience the joys of learning with my students. I know I'm making a real contribution to society by teaching students about the world around them, about faraway places and different times, all while preparing them for their future and careers.

Education

A college degree is a must. I earned my Bachelor's degree in Education at a small community college while I worked part time tutoring middle and high school students. I completed my student teaching requirement during my senior year of college. After graduation, I applied for my teaching certificate and landed my dream job—teaching middle school—not too long after that!

Cool Tools

I get to use the latest technology right inside my classroom. I have an interactive Smart Board in my classroom so that my lessons are more exciting and my students can be actively involved. Education has to change, and technology is leading the revolution. It's exciting that the classroom of the future is developing now.

Financial Factor

I'm sure you've heard someone say that teachers don't teach for the money, meaning, teachers don't make much money. Don't believe it! Teachers may not be getting filthy rich, but teachers make pretty good money! Teachers' salaries depend on a few things: where they teach, how much education they have, and their years' of experience. Even in a private school or a small public school system, with the right combination of experience and education, a teacher can make a good salary. I've been teaching public school for five years now, and my salary is a little over $40,000 a year.

Skills

This could be the job for you if you like working with and helping others and want to make a difference in the world! I'm always up for a challenge, so I look forward to my students' tough questions and I like planning dynamic lessons and teaching material in new ways. I'm a planner and use my time wisely, and I enjoy collaborating and working with my fellow teaching professionals.

If I Could Go Back

I wouldn't! I had to work my way through school because, even though I worked hard and did my best in high school, I didn't make super grades. That doesn't mean I'm not smart...I just don't learn like everyone else, and tests are difficult for me. Needless to say, I had no scholarship offers, and I was raised by a single mom, so you get the picture. It's OK, though, because all of that helps me understand my students.

Initiative

Initiative is definitely a 21st century essential skill. Everyone is so busy, none more so than your teacher or manager. When you have a job, you'll find out just how busy you are with your own job, much less having to help others with theirs, whether you're managing them, on a team, or helping your boss.

It takes experience to be an initiative-taker. You may make a few missteps, but that just goes with the territory. In my opinion, I'd rather have someone who takes initiative than who waits on my every direction for EVERYTHING, even if sometimes they overstep, misunderstand, or otherwise don't quite get it right. (This is not the same as being an "assumer" and never asking questions!)

Taking initiative might involve (just to mention a few things):

- **Anticipating:** Determine what your boss might want or need next, what tools, info, research, reference. This proactive attitude makes you an indispensible right-hand person.

- **Cleaning Up:** When a task is done, there are often many things necessary to wind up the process. Taking initiative to return tools or books, to refile data, to do anything that helps your boss strike out on the next project is a big help. This is just a good exercise in being a team player, showing no job is beneath you, and becoming invaluable.

- **Listening:** Whether you hear what your boss says or read between the lines of an e-mail, you often can ask to do X or Y, clearly seeing that such tasks are coming up. Your boss may wonder if you can read her mind, and appreciate that YOU are the employee who's always on the ball, ahead of the curve, raising their hand, helping facilitate.

This list could go on and on, perhaps expressed as a real world string of common tasks: paving the way, assembling data, building a checklist, asking the right questions, etc. Taking initiative often leads to innovation. Because you are so involved, you may even find you solve some problems, resolve some issues, create some solution so that the job is done before it's even ordered. What do you call that? Magic? It will seem so to your boss. YOU will be ESSENTIAL. You just can't put a price on that (uh, though you might try) when it comes time to pick someone for a promotion or plum job or a leadership role.

Job Title: Nuclear Technician

Success

I hope that I'm a better nuclear technician than Homer Simpson—he does my job in cartoon form, except I'm not lazy or irresponsible…and certainly not yellow. I'm all about safety and use instruments like Geiger counters to monitor radiation levels. As far as I know, none of the people in our power plant have mutated into X-Men or died from radiation poisoning, and I'd like to keep it that way. But really, the health safety aspect of my job is rewarding. I operate machinery and keep a close eye on all aspects of hazardous materials to make sure nobody, in the plant or the public, is exposed to dangerous radiation.

Education

Sometimes you just get lucky. I'd like to say I wanted to be a nuclear technician all my life, but that's not true—I kind of fell into it. I didn't graduate from my high school, but I finally passed the GED and started looking around for something better than lifeguarding at a local pool. I came across a two-year Associate degree in Nuclear Technology and thought, "Yeah, that might be cool." I never liked school before, but I actually enjoyed my classes about chemistry, radiation, and nuclear equipment. After graduation, I landed an entry-level job as an apprentice where I learned the ropes of proper equipment use and instrumentation. I liked that I wasn't expected to be an expert right off the bat.

The Atom Age

Ever since the atomic bomb stunned the world with it's destructive power, people have been looking for better ways to use the atom and perhaps find a sustainable energy source. Because nuclear fusion used for generating power is incredibly dangerous, it's important to have expert technicians like me keeping the public safe from toxic waste and meltdowns.

Financial Factor

Since I'm young and working my way up, I'm earning about $55,000/year, but the average technician makes almost $70,000/year. As my skills improve and I gain more responsibility on the job, my salary will continue to increase. I'm looking long term, and my future is glowing.

Skills

I have lots of responsibilities, first and foremost is monitoring skills—I can't have my head in the clouds while analyzing reaction data or contaminant levels. I also have to evaluate all available information before making decisions, and I'm thinking critically all day long. I listen closely to instructions from scientists and engineers—one wrong step can compromise everyone's safety.

If I Could Go Back

I made life harder on myself by dropping out of school. I was the ringleader of the wrong crowd in high school and liked to skip math class. We all make mistakes, OK, but there came a day when my math skills failed me and I really wished I hadn't built a steep mountain for myself to climb on my way to success.

Grow Your Own Smarts

You can grow your own smarts. You must always increase your knowledge, especially in this fast-moving technological world. Lifelong learning is required. It can be fun!

I was once accused by a savvy fourth-grader of "knowing too much." "No one can know all that stuff," he accused me in front of an auditorium full of students, teachers, principals, media specialists, school board members, and the media. I had just finished holding forth on subjects ranging from Ancient Greece to zombies. He was a very precocious student, the school's "teacher's pet," if you know what I mean. "How do you know all that stuff?" he demanded. Everyone was staring at me, even leaning toward me like in that old E.F. Hutton commercial *("When E.F. Hutton talks...everybody listens.")* It was clear that I had been caught in some awful act of what, exactly, I was not certain—fabricating facts? I abstained from answering for as long as I could. Then I answered in a loud and dramatic voice, leaning down to face my young accuser: **"I READ!"** My audience let out a relieved gasp; the boy nodded agreeably. I had to laugh. How else did they think I knew "all this stuff"? I was baffled, but entertained, by the experience.

To Grow Your Own Smarts...

You can read.

You can take free online classes.

You can take classes of all kinds, even when you can't afford to be fully enrolled in school.

You can take some college classes for free online, and only pay if you pass the test.

You can read.

You can trade learning and skills with a friend: "You tutor me in this and I'll show you how to do that."

You can read.

You can ask your employer to pay for a class in something that helps you do your job.

You can intern for free.

The list is endless. This is not only personal or professional knowledge you will gain, it's personal power. Knowledge is power, as they say. Individual growth is up to you. Achieving competencies and stockpiling skills are real assets that build up your portfolio of job-readiness.

When I met my future son-in-law, he was sitting at his kitchen table, ramrod straight, reading a humongous illustrated science dictionary "for fun." I came across my young production manager sticking pins in an orange. When I looked confounded, he explained, "I'm learning to give shots and do IVs...I want to be a nurse." My husband learned to jump out of airplanes by, imagine this: jumping out of airplanes! Some kids with earbuds in their ears are actually listening to a class. Steve Jobs dropped out of college, but audited free physics classes. I taught my son to type when he was seven (back then you did not learn to type until 10th grade).

Don't kid yourself: Your peers are learning. Don't get left out or left behind. That can happen. Create your own curriculum; it's more fun that way.

Job Title: Crime Scene Technician

Success

I'll bet you've seen CSI: Miami, New York, SVU, or whatever version is on the air these days. Well, my job might not be THAT exciting, nor do I have dark theme music, and my work is never conveniently resolved in a single episode, but it's still a satisfying career that challenges my mental and professional skills—photographing and collecting evidence isn't all that simple, and every case is a huge collaboration. Some of my favorite duties are dusting for fingerprints and searching for DNA evidence. I feel like I'm right in the middle of a "who-done-it" movie, and in some ways, I am. This is real life drama.

Forensics on the Rise

Since scientists started using DNA evidence as substantial proof in courts of law, the criminal justice field has never been the same. It has helped convict felons and free the innocent. Since DNA testing is highly useful and accurate, the field of forensic science is growing up and expected to expand much faster than the average career field in the next ten years.

Skills

What would I be if I weren't observant and good at problem solving? Simple, I'd be a bad crime scene technician. Truly gruesome cases are rare, but in the event, a CST has to be calm, composed, and professional. By the way, you'll want to brush up on your speaking and writing skills—didn't expect that? Communication and documentation is half the job—I can't afford to make mistakes when a person's future rests on my evidence and testimony.

Education

There are many different paths you could take, but all of them involve getting some sort of education: either certification or an Associate or Bachelor's degree in Forensic Science. If you have a specific agency in mind, check their requirements and see what they want in a CST. You'll study all the basic sciences like biology and chemistry while learning the fundamentals of DNA testing, fingerprinting, and evidence collection. Entry-level CSTs receive extensive on-the-job training with a crew of professionals before working on individual cases. For example, DNA analysis training can take six months to a year, and firearms analysis can take up to three years to learn. The good thing is you're not paying for training!

Financial Factor

I've seen many different salaries depending on location. One job posting in a small town stated $40,000–$51,000/year to cover the city and police department, but I saw another posting of $30,000–$42,000/year to cover a whole county. According to the Bureau of Labor Statistics, the average is $51,000/year.

If I Could Go Back

I got an Associate degree before joining a metro investigation unit. I regret not having gone further in my education, maybe advanced into criminology or criminal law.

Junior Achievement

Don't be mistaken—the "junior" in Junior Achievement doesn't mean it's for little kids. It's for YOU! I'm devoting a page to JA because their current goal is to help you be a solution to the workforce skills gap. That means job opportunities for you!

⇨ Did you know?

•79% of companies report a "skills gap" in their organization.
•40–45% of job openings through 2016 will be in middle-skilled occupations, which may only require vocational school or other training, or a two-, not a four-year college degree.

According to employers, here are just some of the "skills" they cannot find in job candidates:

LEADERSHIP SUPERVISORY ABILITY TEAM-BUILDING
GOAL-SETTING PLANNING
MOTIVATION DECISION MAKING ETHICAL JUDGMENT
CREATIVE THINKING PROBLEM SOLVING SELF-DISCIPLINE
SELF-AWARENESS EMPATHY PERSISTENCE
And, believe-it-or-not, TECHNOLOGY SKILLS

Which of these 21st century skills do you posses?
Which could you obtain?
Which will you train for?

Check out Junior Achievement, which has a proven track record of helping you see how to build skills, a powerful pathway from your present to your future, and, besides, it's fun. You can't find your future career if you don't go looking for it.

Junior Achievement®

Job Title: Disaster Management Specialist

Success

My life is a disaster, but not in the usual sense. When Hurricane Katrina hit New Orleans or when the 9/11 terrorist attacks happened, you might have seen the emergency response teams, firefighters, police, and the Red Cross on TV. It is my job to organize those different groups into an intelligent, resourceful emergency response team. I've only been working as a FEMA Disaster Management Specialist for three years, but I worked for the Red Cross in 2005 bringing medical and food supplies to flood victims in New Orleans. It's an exciting job, but it's also about being prepared. I try to avoid meltdowns in my personal life—I stay away from crazy relationships, drive defensively, and avoid buying high-risk stocks—my job is almost the same thing. I advise communities in high-risk areas about how to prepare disaster-proof buildings, or how to protect their citizens in an earthquake. I make emergency response plans, and when a disaster strikes, our plans get put to the test—of mice and men, right? I tell people I wear a helmet to work, and sometimes it's true!

Preparing for the Future

Since September 11, 2001, city governments and businesses have recognized the need for emergency management specialists. Also, weather-related disasters continually strike all over the country, from forest fires out west to the ever-present threats of hurricane season. Or, if you think internationally, cities in Eastern Pacific nations need protection from tsunamis and earthquakes.

Skills

How do you deal with stress? Do you break down and cry, or do you rise to meet the occasion? Managing stress is half the battle. After that you need strong organizational skills and the confidence to mobilize large amounts of people and resources.

Education

Degrees in Emergency Management are now offered at 180 schools across the country. I got my start at the American Red Cross, worked my way up, and then went back to school for my Bachelor's and Master's degrees. Now I work for the Federal Emergency Management Agency (FEMA). Lots of my bosses and mentors got their start in the United States military, working as task organizers and response officers in wartime.

Financial Factor

Pay depends on where you live. A small town government might pay you as little as $28,000/year, while working for the federal government or with a private recovery company could earn you between $70,000–$90,000/year. The average is $50,000.

If I Could Go Back

I would have tried to get an international focus, working in the field of international disaster relief. Too bad I didn't learn another language. Bilingualism opens up doors.

Critical Thinking Skills

Yeah, you hear this term in school all the time, I'm sure. It's hard to have *critical* thinking skills if you don't have thinking skills, so start there. Start with thinking.

We think all the time. (Personally, I'm thinking about the Oreo cookies I know I hid from myself on the top shelf in my kitchen.) To think critically requires some focus. You usually focus on things you care about. I love to watch anyone engaged in forehead-wrinkling, mouth-chewing, one eye-squinting critical thinking, whether it's about a busted transmission, a yearbook layout, the school musical set design, which pizza to order, or, well, whatever. You DO think critically. Think harder. Critical thinking is a required job skill; always has been, always will be. It will be up to YOU to solve the world's problems now. Here are just a few of them; take your choice or invent your own.

(Taken from a "failed legislation" report from a state information site; they all seem to need to be done…maybe they are just waiting for you?)

Design meeting procedures for school boards
Review tax reform effectiveness
Determine the eligibility for National Guard service
Research human embryos
Decide on ignition interlocks for first-time DUI offenders
Create renewable energy resources
Study the methamphetamine issue
Recognize African Americans in Reconstruction
Decide if community colleges can offer BA degrees
Study the shortage of doctors in rural areas
Create new, healthy, affordable desserts
Work on new cancer screening options
Work on new options for organ, eye, and tissue donation
Create a state song
Explore new first job initiatives
Consider a women's history museum
And the list went on and on…

So, here's a Career Recipe:

I would like to ________________________ ___________________________ in/at

___________________________.

Fill in the first blank with *design, explore, create, study, lead, invent…*any other "do" word.
Fill in the second blank with any *task/problem/challenge/opportunity* you wish.
Fill in the third blank with the *name of a place.*

For example: I would like to build robotic prosthetics for children in my own laboratory on a beautiful island.

*Health Science
*Science, Technology, Engineering & Mathematics

Job Title: Genetic Counseling

Success

What's really cool about my job is that the future is wide open. Personally, I specialize in counseling parents of newborns with genetic disorders or birth defects. Often, couples come to me before conception, asking for information on their risks. What I like best is the diversity of daily life: researching family genetics, counseling patients on their options, and helping parents better provide for the needs of their children—this is how I show my passion for people.

Altering the Future

Genetic modification in the food industry has already given us tastier fruits, healthier vegetables, and leaner meat. Human genetic therapy is the new frontier in biological science—it's just a baby science with so much potential. Genetic diseases and disorders can be unhealthy, crippling, or deadly—imagine we can correct those genetic problems by inserting genetic material into existing cells! Realistically, this isn't science fiction.

Skills

Genetic counseling is almost equal parts life science and social service. A healthy interest in science is important, as well as a passion for genetics, but having face-to-face human interaction is the bulk of my responsibilities. I often explain complex technical stuff in plain and simple English, and discuss difficult topics with compassion and tact.

Education

I fell in love with genetics in an advanced biology course while working on a project in drosophila genetics. As an undergraduate student, I majored in biology and psychology. I was horrible in the lab, despite being a good cook—I decided pure research wasn't for me, but I loved genetics and working with people. At the time, the closest Master's degree program in Genetic Counseling was two states away, so I packed my bags! Yes, a Master's degree is required to work, so my suggestion is this: *Try it on and see how it fits.* Don't go into a career that's not going to fulfill your passions.

Financial Factor

A good ballpark figure is $55,000/year. I make additional money by mentoring young counseling professionals in the clinical setting. As with most medical professions, the more you specialize, the fuller your bank account.

If I Could Go Back

Mentors are the most helpful thing anyone can have. I had one professor in my Master's clinical rotation who threw me into new situations with unflinching confidence that I could handle it. I'll admit it was frightening, but he believed in me so strongly, I couldn't bear to disappoint. If I could go back, I would thank all my mentors. A successful person is never successful alone.

Entrepreneurship

I have to give a plug for entrepreneurship. One great thing about being an American is that you can start your own business (as long as it's legal!) at any place at any time at any age!

If money interests you, one way to get rich is to own your own business. That's a fact. It's also a fact that many businesses fail. But many business owners fail, then just start over or pick up where they left off, smarter and even more able to succeed. I know!

The best employee I ever had was able to do, well, *everything*. When I asked her how she knew all about managing, supervising, accounting, marketing, sales, production, shipping, quality control, communicating, and everything else, she said, "I grew up in a family Chinese laundry one-day service business." That explained it! When you own a business you wear all hats, do all things...until you make enough money to hire others.

If you want to be your own boss, you can. Not all of us are cut out to work for others, be a follower instead of a leader, have a set schedule, or get paid what someone else thinks we're worth. NO! Some of us are more than willing, eager, in fact, determined...to lead, work for ourselves, chart our own course, work 24/7/365 if that's what it takes, and earn and achieve all we can on our own terms.

You still will need all the 21st century skills you can gain, all the critical thinking and decision-making smarts you can muster, and a lot of energy. But if you are so inspired, it's easy to be motivated to learn, study, experience, and otherwise prepare yourself to be a business owner.

There are so many things that need to be invented, done, changed, improved, modernized, future-ized in this world, so get busy. Pick one: build something, provide a service, create a product, anything you think people want and need—go for it!

In 1979, I was not happy with the old-style, staid, standoff-ish publishing world. I rebelled and started my own small on-demand press. (Me and about 24,999 other people that year!) I found that I knew a lot but had to learn a lot more. It was hard, fun, adventurous, and eventually, successful. My career path took me to all 50 states and around the world. I made a lot of money. I had a lot of fun. The other day I emailed my editorial assistant to ask if I had already written the "entrepreneur" page for this book or not. She emailed back: "Look up the word in the dictionary—it has your picture beside it!"

That might be the nicest business compliment I ever got. Dive on in to the entrepreneurial life, the water's fine!

Job Title: Speech-Language Pathologist

Success

Communication is a basic human need. It's truly something special, magical even, when a child or adult can suddenly, without fear, communicate and unlock what's inside. More people have speech problems than you might think, especially in early childhood. It's a fulfilling career because irregular speech patterns as a child, if not diagnosed and resolved, can grow into big problems for an adult. I know sign language, and it's kind of funny how much time I spend sticking out my tongue, teaching students how to make sounds or how to exercise their voices—I love making my students crack up laughing.

Career Options

With a speech-language pathology degree and certification, you'll be qualified to work in several different environments. Almost 50 percent work in a school setting, like I do, but you can find work in a hospital or clinic doing speech recovery therapy, in the offices of physical, occupational, and speech therapists, or in nursing care facilities. In this career, you'll work with a wide range of patients from children to persons suffering from a stroke or cleft palate.

Skills

The inability to communicate is so frustrating you want to rip something up. I understand that, so I'm sure to exercise compassion, patience, and moral support. I'm always thinking and analyzing, trying to find creative, effective ways to produce results, and I owe it to my patients to listen intensely and document all details of their cases.

Education

My decision to become a speech-language pathologist is somewhat personal. As a young adult, I stuttered terribly. I would get stuck on a word like a skipping record, or like someone threw a crowbar into the gears in my mouth—it just wouldn't come out. A speech pathologist helped me get over that. After all the trouble of getting a Bachelor's degree in History, I became a full-time parent (not the best-paying job), but as soon as my kids were old enough, a friend suggested I go back to school for a two-year, speech-language pathology Master's degree program. I took one class to whet my appetite, and then found myself diving in headfirst! Like most health and counseling professions, this one requires certification, and sometimes a period of supervised clinical experience—believe me, you'll want all the help you can get!

Financial Factor

The pay range is anywhere between $42,000 and $110,000/year. Working in an elementary school, I earned $57,000 for nine months of work, meaning I get three months off for school holidays and summer vacation. Keep in mind that the more experience you have, the higher your salary will climb.

If I Could Go Back

I love school. I would go back in a heartbeat if it had something to go back for. I don't want a career change, but if I ever get tired of treating speech disorders, I'll gladly stick my nose back in the books.

Success Does Not Come to the Wimpy

Read that headline again. I have a sign on the wall in my CEO office with those words on it.

I love the early Coast Guard lifesavers' motto: *"You don't have to come back, you just have to go out."*

Getting a job is just the beginning of your career. Learning as many 21st century skills in advance is a real advantage because you will be using them every day. Business moves very fast these days. Change is constant. Opportunity and success come to those who are brave enough to volunteer, speak up, ask for an assignment, try something different out of their comfort zone, be creative, and otherwise help their new company move forward.

Business is not about sitting still. It does not come in neat, tidy packets like quarters or semesters. "Tests" are not announced; they come every day in the way you handle yourself, do your job, ask questions, think, solve problems, handle ambiguity, and many other things.

You will fail. You will have embarrassing moments. It's OK; you're new. Your boss may be patient as you learn the ropes—but not for long. The "scorekeeping" system for business is numbers and dates: profit or loss, and deadlines. Quality control is not a theory…it's a constant goal, and zero defects means just that—no errors, please.

Excuses are not especially tolerated. Even the nicest boss is not your mom, dad, or best friend. You might be surprised not to get much credit for just showing up, being on time, dependability, and such—these are just givens. Respect will be gained as you show what you can and will do, how fast you learn, how adroit you are at adapting, and how much you really care about your job, not just "playing" at your job.

To strike out for the territory of your future is exciting, and scary. The more you treat school and home with earnestness and responsibility, the easier you can move down the path into your career, and then onward and upward. Don't be afraid. Remember, success does not come to the wimpy!

**Marketing, Sales & Service*
**Arts, Audio/Video Technology & Communications*

Job Title: Social Media Manager

Success

In the last decade, social media websites exploded—and consequently, changed how businesses think. My job didn't exist ten years ago, but now it's alive and thriving. Because the business game is always evolving, I use my experience with social media outlets like Facebook, Twitter, LinkedIn, and blogs to give companies a face in the media world. Right now, I'm working for CNN in Atlanta to explore emerging news outlets and faster ways to spread breaking news. I really have an amazing, challenging job—a digital-age combination of public relations, content creation (media writing, blogging, tweeting), and business development. I hate to brag, but I'm the whole package.

Social Revolution

Social media is revolutionizing the way people communicate and showing off in unexpected ways. And as if to prove its importance, social media had a huge role in the political uprisings in the Middle East by allowing people to connect, spread ideas, and join together to overthrow whole governments. This is powerful stuff. Get connected!

Skills

"Well rounded" is a good description of a social media manager. Are you a computer geek AND a candid people person? You must be creative, patient, and responsive—no holing up in a dark room when something goes wrong. Think like a journalist, but have the business and communication savvy of a public relations guru. And most importantly, you'll go far on your passion for social media.

Education

Since this is such a new, emerging and socially "now" career, the education requirements are not well defined. Social media managers come from all walks of life, and many companies look for a candidate with a Bachelor's degree in English, Journalism, and Media Communications, or Business Management and Marketing. But listen for a moment—education doesn't always get you the job. Experience is key, and you can start on your own. Anyone can be on Facebook and Twitter, but my suggestion is this: use social media outlets in a special way to build a "social portfolio." For example, if you are interested in fashion, you could start your own blog about fashion, create a Facebook group that keeps abreast of fashion trends and historic fashion icons, and start a LinkedIn profile to create a professional network. An employer wants to see that you're responsible, passionate and active in the social world, not just reposting funny cat memes.

Financial Factor

It depends on where you work. A small start-up company might pay $30,000/year, while working for a multi-national corporation could pay upwards of $90,000/year.

If I Could Go Back

My first job was with a small town wedding magazine, and I learned a lot on-the-job, but I honestly believe a degree in media communications could have saved me pain.

Tune in to Your Network

While you might end up working anywhere around the world, don't underestimate the opportunities right out your own back door. If you go online and check out the top companies in our state, you will find that they just might be anywhere. Also, if you checked the bios of the top 100 business leaders in the state, you might also find that they came from almost anywhere in the state, from the tiniest town to the largest cities.

Everyone has to start somewhere and while it's great to bloom where you are planted, it's also possible to find your first local job leading you to a different branch or plant or other location in the state, region, nation, or another country.

People move, businesses move. Do yourself a great favor and start a networking notebook. You don't actually have to have someone's business card. Just make a list of all the people you meet over the years: teachers, ministers, parents' friends, people you worked for (even while in school), fellow students, etc. Over time, as you move around and they do too, you'll be surprised how often you might encounter one another, recommend one another—it's like building your own special club of smart, savvy, helpful friends.

"Word of mouth" is a real asset. When you do good work, people are glad to recommend you. You, yourself, might one day seek talent from fine people you've met or worked with in the past. Don't burn bridges behind you. Always take the high road, do the right thing, and leave relationships on a good note. All that might sound like corny, old-fashioned advice, until one day when you find that grouchy teacher you were respectful to wrote you a great letter of recommendation, or that acquaintance you went to community college with ends up being the personnel director for a company where you're seeking a position.

It's also very common that when someone starts a new business venture, they often seek smart, talented, honest, capable people they have met in the past to join them. The possibilities are endless!

Job Title: Physical Therapist

Success

I think I have the best job in America. Really. It's very satisfying, or maybe I should say gratifying. I feel like my work is beneficial to my patients and society. Regularly, I diagnose a patient's condition, project a plan for recovery, and then work my hardest to get that person back to physical, and sometimes emotional, health. It's like giving a person his or her life back, and that's what I enjoy most.

Special Cases

Some of the most heart-wrenching cases I've encountered are stroke victims who have lost partial use of their motor functions. One of my patients was referred to me with paralysis on the right side of her body and an almost complete loss of speech. The road to recovery is long, but I collaborated with a speech pathologist to combine nerve stimulation, massage, and speech therapy. When she spoke again, the first thing she said to us was "thank you."

Skills

I have a strong desire to help people and compassion is my strongest tool—understanding and being a friend in a time of weakness. Likewise, you should have interpersonal skills—that means you get along with people just fine. And the other side is physical, like giving manual therapy with your hands and doing a good deal of physical lifting.

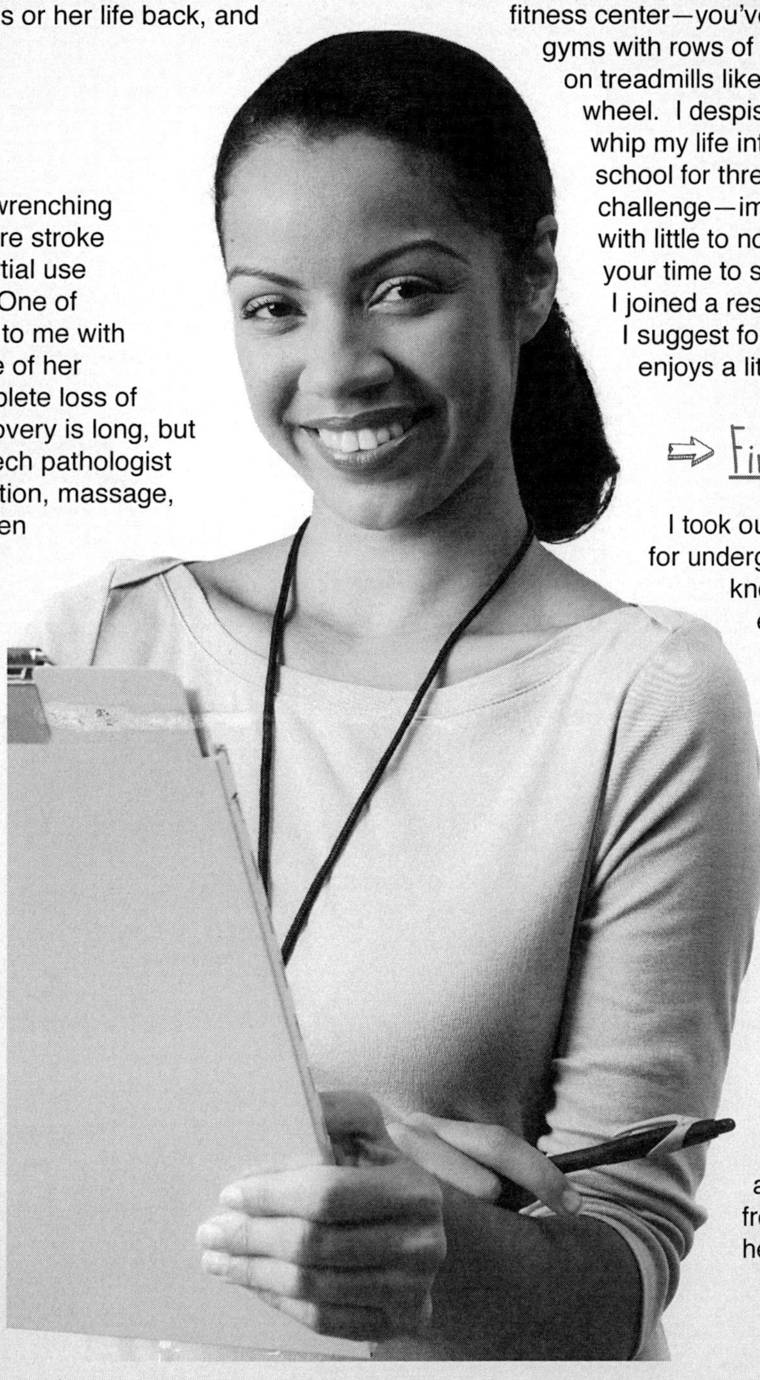

Education

For better or worse, this profession requires a postgraduate professional degree, that means being a doctor, specifically a Doctor of Physical Therapy (DPT). Doctoral programs require a Bachelor's degree for admission and last about three years. I studied biology in college, but ended up as a manager in a chain fitness center—you've seen the equipment-filled gyms with rows of sweaty, breathless people on treadmills like gerbils on an exercise wheel. I despised my job, so I decided to whip my life into shape. I went back to school for three years for my DPT, a real challenge—imagine going back to school with little to no income and dedicating all your time to studying. After graduation, I joined a residency program, which I suggest for anyone who, like me, enjoys a little extra guidance.

Financial Factor

I took out about $100,000 in loans for undergrad and graduate school—I know, that's a lot. But since I earn a little more than the average, about $80,000/year, I can afford to pay back those loans in a few years. I'll be happy when they aren't hanging over my head anymore.

If I Could Go Back

I might have considered being a personal trainer, but nothing quite gives me the same job satisfaction as helping people recover from an injury and maintain healthy lifestyle changes.

Work Words to Know

While there are many work words to learn, here are just a few you might really want to know! (They may even sound familiar from school.)

Performance-based: Most jobs these days have nothing to do with your age or longevity with the company. Businesses reward consistent good performance; make sure yours is.

Results-oriented: Business rewards people who achieve measurable results, whether that's increased sales or revenues, improved efficiency, lowered costs, or creativity that produces new products or processes. Never take on a task or assignment without considering the results you are to achieve.

Solutions: Really, work is about solving problems—big problems, small problems. The person who can use their critical thinking skills to solve problems is invaluable in business. Practice problem-solving.

You don't have to wait until the world of work to practice achieving a good performance and excellent, measurable results, or solving problems. This is what responsible adults do all day long. Move along on this spectrum and your future schooling, your first job, and your career will be much easier.

Job Title: Strong Motion Seismologist

Success

Most seismologists are pessimistic about accurately predicting earthquakes, but that doesn't mean we can't better prepare for earth-shaking disasters. I'm working in an important subfield of the earthquake sciences called strong motion seismology. I use accelerometer sensors to record seismic motion strong enough to cause structural collapse and ground failures such as landslides and earth flows. Our goal is to provide lawmakers and construction engineers with accurate information about the motion of fault lines and how to prepare for major shifts in the earth's crust.

Education

The best undergraduate education path for seismologists is in geophysics. Unfortunately, I wasn't accepted to a school with a geophysics program. Instead, I got my Bachelor's degree in Earth and Atmospheric Sciences. One of my best experiences was being a research intern under a geophysicist recording and mapping seismic activity on the west coast. It was great to travel for fieldwork and get hands-on experience with the seismometer equipment. Some seismologists can lasso a job with a Bachelor's degree, but most seismologists who want to record and interpret data need to go on to a doctoral program, usually in geophysics. Remember that field experience is the most important. Work with people already established as seismologists, make connections, and wriggle into the place you want to be. That's what I did.

Coming Soon

Earthquakes, tsunamis, and volcanoes are all disasters that fall in the field of seismology. The science of prediction is far from accurate, but seismologists are more concerned with preparing for the inevitable disaster coming soon. Strong motion seismology also plays a life-saving role by predicting aftershock tremors in the wake of an initial shock.

Financial Factor

The salary range is wide, from $30,000 to $110,000/year. OK, let's break that down by averages: state government seismologists earn about $57,000/year, federal government seismologists earn approximately $91,000/year, technical consulting firms pay seismologists close to $61,000/year, and seismologists in the oil industry earn upwards of $100,000/year.

Skills

Start with a healthy interest in physics, math, and earth science. You must be extremely capable of reading and interpreting data, but also remember you can know all there is to know about earthquakes, but without computer skills and basic programming capability, that knowledge can't be applied.

If I Could Go Back

Don't take this the wrong way—I think my job is socially important, and I enjoy my work, but the tasks can be lonely and isolating. Even though my colleagues are a down-to-earth group, if I could go back, I might consider a job where I could see more faces every day.

Positive Assets

Here are just a few things employers really appreciate and respond to:

a positive attitude

being attuned to new trends

boundless energy

good writing and speaking skills

encouraging and empowering others

being innovative, efficient, loyal, and dedicated

inspired by challenges to seek creative solutions

the ability to self-critique and improve oneself

seeing obstacles as opportunities

challenging "foolish consistencies"

authenticity, genuineness

being inclusive and tolerant

self-motivation and purposefulness

perseverance

Have something to bring to the table, because that will make you more welcome.

—Randy Pausch, *The Last Lecture*

Job Title: Freelance Writer

Success

Don't let anyone fool you with that "starving artist" old wives' tale—a good writer can make a good living, as can a good artist, but I can't draw a straight line. The best way to become a freelance writer is to CARE about people, places, things, words, and everything else. Sometimes I can't recall my phone number, but I can reel off details about zombies, pirates, the American Revolution, Julia Child, the history of the Olympics, and endless other things. I like to say my specialty is "everything" if you want it told in plain English with wit, charm, and enthusiasm. Most folks like that because they want people to read what they pay me to write.

A Good Background

You should start preparing to be a writer about as soon as you are born. Really, everything you read, learn, see on television, in movies, and on the web will come in handy at some point. Self-education is great—I study English and literature, naturally, but history, science, and everything else, even math, which, honestly, is not my strong suit. I collect good books too and I'm very picky—books are hard to move around, you know?

Skills

Discipline is the most important skill for a writer. Surprised? You can't meet your deadlines if you don't truly have a schedule and live up to it. I write sick, well, early, late, and all night if I must. The other required skill is just doing a great job. A writer can't hide; your words really do speak for you. And if you always "bring it" on time and professionally, word of mouth will do your advertising work for you.

Education

I'm a self-taught writer, meaning I didn't go to college and get a degree. I took a lot of classes, but mostly I started writing in elementary school and on every school newspaper or anything I could volunteer for. My Dad was in the Rotary Club and I used to write news releases and short items for him, and when he told his friends who had written that "great article," they asked for my help too. I did a lot for free, but it gave me confidence, bylines, contacts, and published articles to show. My education today is to immerse myself in my subject; my goal is to bring up details that even the person who hired me doesn't know. That "wows 'em" every time!

Money

You have to be disciplined as a freelancer, setting aside for your taxes and expenses. I'm not cheap at all, but fair, and good at managing my money so that it's one less thing to worry about. I need all my time for writing. That being said, the average salary for writers is between $30,000 and $50,000/year.

If I Could Go Back

Hmm, I think I might have gotten a college degree, but in a specific subject, not writing—say history or science, since that's what I specialize in writing about.

Don't Be Discouraged

It would be a grave mistake for you to do either of the following:

a. figure that adults have messed up the world so badly that there's no fixing it;
b. assuming that all the problems that need solving will be done by others.

YOU are the future; we really are counting on you.

Yes, as I write this, there are many problems in education, the environment, world politics, the economy, and more. But every era has plenty of problems to solve, and, guess what? It's YOUR turn to shine!

If there are to be future leaders, future educators, future health care providers, future inventors, future entrepreneurs, future figure-it-outers and fixer-uppers, it has to be you!

The knowledge, experiences, and skills you are gathering now are the tools and talents you will bring to bear on all the issues that face us. While some problems are obvious, and some solutions are typical, the future is very exciting. The odds are that you will have a job, or jobs, one day that do not even exist now, that do not even have a name…so it's hard for me to talk about them.

One way to get a good feeling for this transition is to read history, and especially biographies of innovators, inventors, and entrepreneurs. It is very exciting to see how they took tough times and made them better, observed apparently insurmountable problems and solved them, and even better yet, just invented something cool—like the light bulb, telephone, airplane, or first personal computer. (Thank goodness for that invention!)

YOU are the person who will build the better mousetrap, invent the new medicine, cure the dreaded disease, advance the economy through better banks, transportation, schools, equipment, manufacturing, communication, materials, systems, strategies, colors, fabrics, tools, sounds, music…you keep adding the words.

Where you see irresponsibility, you can change things. You can make the inefficient efficient, the broken repaired, the unreliable reliable, the old-fashioned/outmoded/outdated…newfangled and wonderful.

Hey, hurry it up, will ya?

Job Title: Purchasing Agent/Buyer

Success

In some ways this is a glamorous, powerful career—I'm a chief wheeler-dealer, but all the glitz might cloud the hard work and sharp intellect needed to succeed in this competitive career. I got my start as a salesperson for Nike, but now I'm a buyer for a specialty shoe distributor. I consider availability and marketability, negotiate prices, and close on deals. Business is risky, and big risks are bank or bust—buying is as close to gambling as you can get. For example, who would have bet Snuggies would sell? Or Crocs, for that matter?

Side Business

My grandma bought things—so what? She hoards them too. When I was young, she took me to yard, garage, and estate sales to buy antique furniture, old coins, toys, lamps, and anything else that looked valuable. With my confidence as a buyer, I opened a side business buying and reselling odds-and-ends. This might not seem like a moneymaker, but I've really worked into something good. I travel all over Europe to home closings and auctions, looking for treasures to buy cheap and resell at a higher price. It's an addiction, I know, but finding the perfect buy is like being a kid at Christmas. (Thanks, Grandma!)

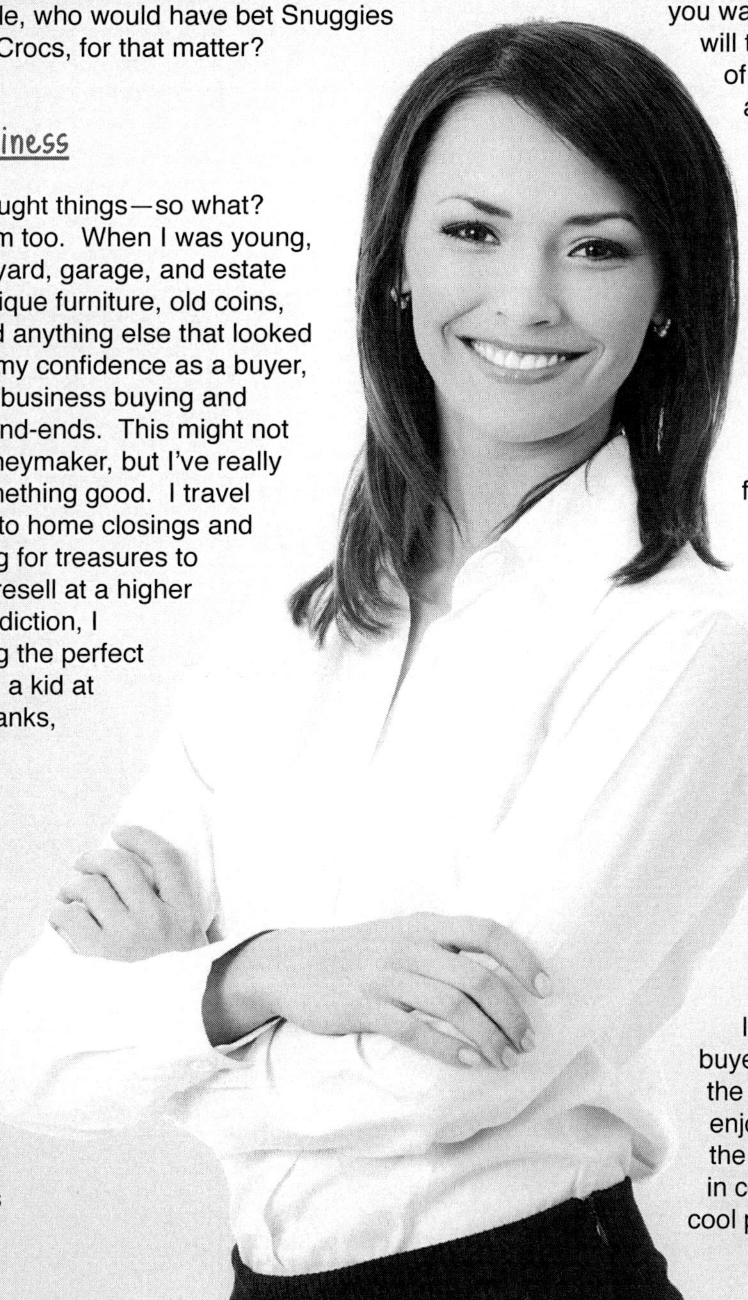

Skills

Negotiation is the key word for good buyers. You really have to drive a hard bargain or there are sellers that'll eat you alive. Don't be taken for a fool. Your job is to buy at the best price, make quick judgments, and smart partnerships with suppliers. Also, professional buyers are usually in touch with the specific taste and trends of their specific field. For example, a buyer of books might have studied English literature.

Education

How much you hit the textbooks depends on where you want to work. Some small companies will train entry-level buyers straight out of high school. Other larger stores and distributors require Bachelor's or Master's degrees in Business—there are plenty of certifications you'll want to check out too. I took business classes at a community college, and to pay the bills, I worked in sales. I like learning on-the-job because you get to see real people do the job well. If you stay in the field, purchasing agents usually move up to management positions or become buyers of larger wholesale products for major distribution.

Financial Factor

A buyer's salary is in the neighborhood of $50,000/year. With experience comes higher pay, and working your way into a purchasing manager position will net you closer to $90,000/year. You can buy a lot with that kind of money!

If I Could Go Back

I might have foregone the career as a buyer. While a steady salary is nice, I like the freedom of my side business better. I enjoy the global traveling experience and the importing of foreign goods brings me in contact with really fascinating people in cool places.

The New Look of Business

You are advancing through school, higher education, and into the work world at a very exciting time. Once "work" pretty much took place in a factory, or in an office at a desk. But today, as you well know, the virtual world, the Internet, and social media are changing things very, very rapidly.

Not only will you participate in these changes (so get ready!), you may even create the new ways and means we learn, study, communicate, and do business. Young workers have an advantage here since you have grown up with technology, you "get it," and you like it.

However, your next challenge will be to learn how to harness technology, help it solve problems and create new ways of doing things. Everyday, new things get old. This happens faster and faster. You don't have to write code to be part of this amazing revolution continuing to happen just as you are becoming an adult able to help speed things along more interestingly, effectively, and inventively.

Now is NOT the time to avoid science, math, technology studies, or anything that will help you as you discover that YOU may be your office…that you may work with a team spread out around the world…that time zones are irrelevant—and that as a consumer, student, employee, and most anything else you are or set out to be—that your ability to be successful is in great part dependent on your ability to keep up with the fast-changing technological advances.

We ask, "Is there an app for that?" YOU may be the app!

Job Title: Lean Specialist

Success

My job is to make a company efficient, streamlined, and optimized—all the extra fat cut off—lean. Businesses hire me to revamp their production processes, business strategies, and internal management. What I like best about my work is doing more with less—achieving critical results, fast and consistently, and busting through metrics like there's no tomorrow.

Lean

A while back, Toyota developed a process that revolutionized business production. The concept and application of these production processes and principles became known as "Lean." Although not every business uses the lean production model, many companies are renovating their procedures inside and out by hiring trained professionals like me to cut costs, increase production, and get results.

Skills

In superhero form, my critical thinking skills look like The Hulk. I'm solution-oriented and can crunch numbers in my head without breaking a sweat. And believe it or not—I'm actually a people person! I like to enter a company and make friends first. Nobody likes a newcomer coming in and messing everything up. Explanation of my actions is highly important for cooperation and smooth transition.

Education

The most direct route to becoming a process analyst is to get education and training. I studied business in college, and minored in accounting. I made good connections through my professors and showed up at job fairs, eventually landing an entry-level job, as an assistant under a senior business process analyst. I was overwhelmed with the work, and almost quit my job. I explained to my supervisor that I wasn't paid enough to be doing all that work, and he said, "Pay your dues now. It'll pay off later." It's also where I first heard about the lean process. My advice for your education is this: You'll never stop learning in this job, so keep your resume up-to-date, and keep your wits about you!

Financial Factor

Pay off, it did. Some process analysts make upwards of \$100,000/year—that's a big-time, process guru salary. I make around \$58,000/year, but I'm okay with that. I'm young, and as my experience grows, so will my salary.

If I Could Go Back

Honestly, a resume doesn't get you a job. I had a great college resume, good grades, and plenty of extracurricular activities, but companies wouldn't look at me without work experience. I would have taken a summer job, or been a babysitter—something, anything work-related to brag about.

Strategies for Skill-Building

- •Take all the classes you can
- •Watch for inexpensive or free community classes
- •Trade out mentoring: "You teach me this and I'll teach you that."
- •Online classes are available around the world and around the clock, many are free
- •Find a class in job search
- •Take classes in specific skills: resume writing, improved study habits, finding a scholarship
- •Take classes to explore interests: Spanish, CPR, website-building
- •Take classes to network
- •Check school and public libraries for classes
- •Join local clubs whether Rotary, or other, where businesspeople belong
- •Volunteer for almost anything
- •Teach Sunday School, swimming, chess, anything—and add that to your resume
- •Take a creative class if you struggle with that, whether art, creative writing, or anything outside of your comfort zone
- •Take a speaking class; Toastmasters offers them
- •Check out your local Chamber of Commerce; ask to sit in or audit a business meeting or class or panel discussion
- •Do as many short internships as you can
- •Work as many part-time jobs over time as you can
- •Help anyone; learning about one kind of work is always beneficial to seeing how it applies to another type of work

The opportunities are endless. When all else fails, read a book (real, electronic, or other) or, write one!

Add it all to your resume!

Job Title: Cytotechnologist

Success

I might be a shy person, but I'm proud to say that I'm the first line of defense against cancer. I'm not looking for the cure—my job is more practical. As a cytotechnologist, I am trained to detect cancerous and precancerous cells, lesions, and abnormalities. A pathologist depends on me to analyze cellular material, determine its health, and make the initial diagnosis. I like to complain that I slave over a hot microscope all day, but I think what I do is pressingly important and necessary—I really love knowing that if I make a diagnosis early enough, there's a good chance to cure a patient.

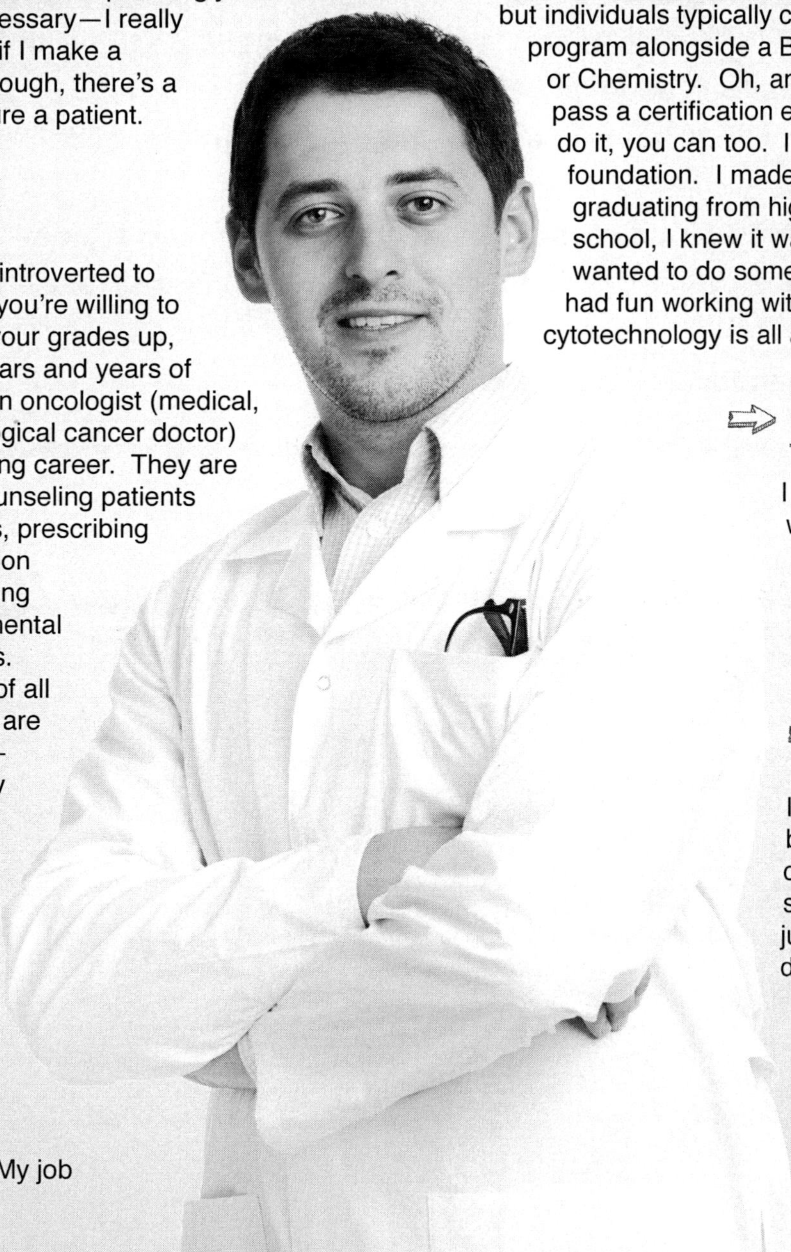

Oncology

I was too shy and introverted to be a doctor, but if you're willing to study hard, keep your grades up, and go through years and years of schooling, being an oncologist (medical, surgical, or radiological cancer doctor) is a highly rewarding career. They are responsible for counseling patients about their options, prescribing medicine or radiation therapy, and keeping abreast of experimental treatment methods. About 25 percent of all deaths in the U.S. are related to cancer—what does that say about the demand for oncologists?

Skills

I am proud to say that I know the appearance and function of every cell in the human body. My job sometimes feels tedious and monotonous, but I owe it to each patient to be meticulous and detail-oriented with each slide. Also, confidence in working independently and an interest in science and lab work are good vital signs for this career.

Education

A solid foundation in high school sciences is the first step. After that, cytotechnology programs offered by either universities or hospitals last one to two years, but individuals typically complete a cytotechnology program alongside a Bachelor's degree in Biology or Chemistry. Oh, and after all that, you'll need to pass a certification exam. But don't worry, if I can do it, you can too. I'll remind you, start with a good foundation. I made sure to have good grades graduating from high school. Looking at medical school, I knew it was beyond my financial reach. I wanted to do something focused on diseases—I had fun working with microscopes, and that's what cytotechnology is all about!

Financial Factor

I make around $69,000/year working in a private lab—that's better than average. Workers in hospitals generally get a lower but the trade-off is that you'll wider variety of patients.

If I Could Go Back

I'm not really a people person, but I think it's important that cytotechnologists think about the slides as individual persons, not just random slides. Back in the day, cytotechnologists had more patient interaction, but now the high volume of slides means that we've lost the patient connection—I'd like to see that change in the future.

The Entrepreneurial Edge

Not everyone is destined to be an entrepreneur, but starting your own business is one of the most exciting things you can do!

Just so you'll know:

- **You don't have to make a product; you can provide a service**
- **You don't have to have any money to start most businesses**
- **The Small Business Administration is full of free, clear advice**
- **Working for a short time in the kind of business you'd like to start is helpful**
- **Working in a small business where you might wear many hats is instructive**
- **You can do an online business in your spare time and still go to school**
- **A business plan, even one page, is a big help**
- **Your local community may have coaching and other help for a budding entrepreneur**
- **Lunch and learn: Invite a businessperson to lunch—fast food is fine—and ask if you can pick his or her brain; they'll probably be flattered (and possibly pay for lunch!)**
- **Find a smart friend and start a partnership**

Even if your fledgling start-up crashes and burns, that's part of the entrepreneurship experience. Try again!

Job Title: Software Developer

Success

I'll say it loud and proud that I'm a computer nerd, and my career is one of the best-paid, in-demand, jobs in America. We are the creative minds that nurture a new software product from concept through its development cycle to a final release. I work with code programmers, design flowcharts, check for runtime errors, and optimize efficiency. I specialized in Java development, and am working for a development company.

Video Game Developers

Video game development is an ensemble affair with software developers right in the heart of it. It's an interesting career to explore, with lots of different ways to use your computer skills. Some of my closest friends from college have really enjoyed working for companies like Ubisoft in Montreal, Canada, and attended big conventions like E3.

Skills

Despite the computer nerd stereotype, software developers are usually well-rounded people. I, for one, have great teamwork and customer service skills, as well as being the creative and dynamic force behind our new product development. It goes without saying that technical computer skills (operating systems, programming languages, design tools, etc.) are the bulk of what you'll learn in school, but being analytical and a problem solver are the qualities you want to start with.

Education

Growing up, I had my hands glued to a computer most of the time anyway, so I thought, why not do something with it? I was no genius in high school—I didn't even apply myself to 4-H or Spanish Club. After high school, I waited tables to pay my way through a junior college. A technical computing course in Java language really sparked my interest, and that's when I decided to go on to get my Bachelor's degree in Computer Science. I relied on loans and scholarships to get me through it. Other degrees available for software developers are software engineering and even mathematics. Be sure to take classes that focus on software development and computer languages, because that's what will apply to an actual job.

Financial Factor

Yes indeed, the average software developer earns $90,000/year. At first, I had trouble finding an entry-level job and worked odd jobs for two years, but when I did land a software development position, I started out around $60,000/year and quickly received pay raises in the following years.

If I Could Go Back

Working odd jobs was actually fairly fun. I stayed active as a painter in a construction crew, and I enjoyed being a pet-sitter until a dachshund bit my ankle. It's not like I was making any real income, but I liked being able to try new things all the time.

"It's Gonna Be a Bumpy Ride!"

Every year, I start the year with a blog to my employees. It may be helpful to you to see what's on my mind. FYI: This blog came with an attachment of a long "wish list" of things I wanted for the year, related to jobs, work, new products, revenue numbers, and such. Truly, work is lead, follow, or get out of the way!

The Future is So Yesterday!

Duh? Huh? Oh, yeah, folks, believe me! The future is so yesterday.

When did this happen? I suppose when we weren't looking. At the turn of the century, we had a clue that the future (a.k.a. the Twenty-first Century) was coming, but we have already passed the first decade of that event boundary.

Today there is a mechanical heart that whirrrrrrrs blood through your veins via spinning blades—no motor and no heartbeat required! Books have given way to e-Bibles, e-comics, and e-everything else. New planets the size and approximate atmosphere of Earth are being discovered. Dreaded cancer IS curable in many instances. And more, so much more.

This all is on my mind because I run a business. Last year, I described employees (mine and others) as being either Old-Fashions or Newfangles. The differences were clear. This year I feel the import of such distinctions even more clearly. You are either part of the past, or, as Buzz Lightyear might say, "To infinity and beyond."

I can tell that the future has already come and gone because so many Newfangles now start up businesses with no baggage of the past. They enter the economic fray already up to speed and, indeed, beyond, taking everything to the next, new new level.

I have always been a futurist, in spite of the fact that I live a big chunk of my life in the past in my involvement with social studies. But nothing about how that history curriculum now gets done has anything to do with the past. Today you either work at the speed of light or get left behind.

My job is to create, and often those creations have no name. That hinders me not and should not hinder or stymie those charged with helping me. So don't be an Old-Fashion, be a Newfangle. We don't want to eat our competitors' e-dust, do we?

Yes, the future is so yesterday. I'm not sure what we're in now, but as Betty Davis once said in a movie, "It's gonna be a bumpy ride."

The best way to predict the future is to invent it.
—Alan Kay

Job Title: Executive Assistant

Success

I don't know how many times I've heard, "I couldn't live without you!" My boss, the CEO of a small company, would be helpless without me in the office to prepare memos, reports, letters, and invoices, while also wrangling all the crazy projects in our office. And that's not all I do—not by a long shot. I also manage my boss's personal affairs like booking travel reservations and contacting realtors. Sounds like a lot of thankless work, right? Sometimes things get hectic and my desk becomes a hazard zone, but at the end of the day, I love my job.

Knowledge•Experience

This is the combo every employer is looking for, and an executive assistant needs both, including clerical knowledge (expertise in office software programs, recording and filing, form design, etc.) and customer service knowledge. Experience is especially valuable when handling delicate situations.

Skills

I swear sometimes I talk like I'm scatterbrained, but I promise, I'm not. My organization skills save my life every day—it's my job to sort people, tasks, and correspondence into the proper places at the proper times. I'm an easygoing talker and listener with a supreme sense of priority, which helps me maintain sanity. And you might be surprised that relationship skills are gold. I understand my boss better than she knows herself.

Education

Like I said before, this job is all about knowledge and experience. No college degree required, but you'll need the basic computer and processing skills. Getting your foot in the door is the most important part. If you can get that first job as a secretary or assistant, most of your training will be on-the-job experience—you'll make mistakes, but that's what learning is all about. I actually have a college degree in communications, but I faced a terrible job market and took a secretary job at a gas gauge company. Working there for two years gave me the knowledge and experience I needed to become an executive assistant.

Financial Factor

Like many jobs that don't require a college education, you'll start out low, gain necessary skill and experience, and then make good money. I started out making $29,000/year as a secretary at that gas gauge company, but as an executive assistant, I've moved up to about $45,000/year. Like many jobs, your financial factor depends on where you live. A family member of mine just took an executive assistant job in a big, West Coast city and will be bringing home $60,000.

If I Could Go Back

Oh goodness, I don't know. I'm too busy to look back. Many students overlook the importance of basic math skills, or business classes for that matter. You can make your life easier by learning those things while you're young, or learn the hard way. It's your choice.

A Craftsman by Design

Paul La Brosse dropped out of high school when he was 14 to work in construction with his uncles. At age 11, someone had told him (in front of his friends), "You have the hands of an artist!"; he was not too happy about that. As a young adult, a woman told him the same thing: "You have the hands of an artist."

Paul is the person we all want to be. According to him, "I can't wait to get up in the morning and get to work!" The delighted twinkle (really, a real twinkle!) in his eyes lets you know that this is true. Like many boys of his generation, Paul learned by doing. His was a true on-site apprentice with men who had been building things all their lives. No book could have taught him the fine nuances of the magic formula of technical + creative that leads to the construction of everything from doghouses to cathedrals.

Paul was no dummy; he picked the brains of everyone he met, especially one builder who was a true old-world craftsman. "Even at lunch," Paul says, "I'd just ask question after question. Why did you do that? How do you do this? I was always very inquisitive."

Inquisitive. Such an essential skill! How do you learn anything if you aren't interested, if you don't care? You don't.

Paul is working on my house. He is tall, all muscle, and sports a charming unruly head of black hair. He's a lot older than you are. But Paul has the best job in the world. By his own admittance: "I do what I love and I love what I do!"

One day, Paul brought his portfolio of projects for me to see. I was amazed, truly amazed. He's a genius. Imagine designing and constructing buildings that have no straight lines, just angles, and getting to work from the original blueprints of famous architect Frank Lloyd Wright. Paul built a chapel that has walls that float like marshmallow clouds. He took a mountain of old, gnarled, bent and beat-up boards destined for the trash heap and built the loveliest horse barn imaginable. When he needed a single piece of wood to be curved into a beautiful staircase for a historic home, he soaked the wood in his pond (as he cooled off!) and molded it into the perfect shape. "I love using my technical skills and my creativity," Paul says. "I love a challenge and enjoy doing the impossible." Those eyes twinkle.

My point in sharing Paul's story is that only you can find the pathway to your life's work. In spite of this book and all you will hear from adults, there are not nearly as many rules as you think. Paul had plenty of people who suggested he get a "real job." But he did not let anyone deter him from his dream; nor should you.

They call it a job track or a career pathway because, like Paul's lovely staircase, it's not a straight line. The twists and turns, unexpected angles, and even "dropping out" can all add up to a beautiful, fun, productive, lucrative career that you will be proud of. Don't let anyone tell you differently.

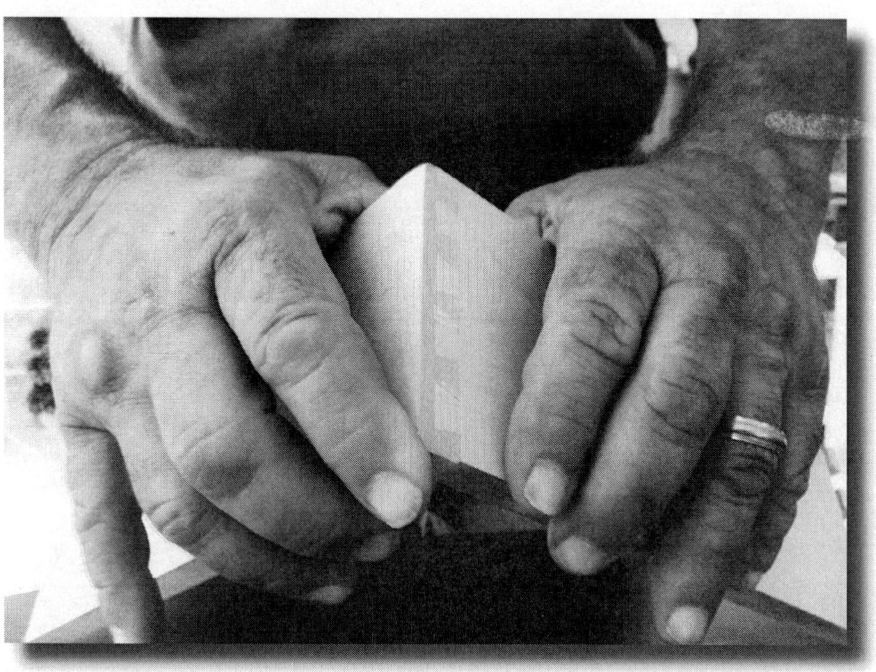

Intern Biography

Name: Charles Peterson

Born: 1989 in Boulder, Colorado
High School: Graduated from Newnan High School in Newnan, Georgia
College: Mercer University in Macon, GA
Since then: World traveler, volunteer teacher, and Gallopade intern
Future: Undecided and happy to explore

I'm like you—young and unsure exactly what I'll be doing in 10 years. I think young people, at least on some level, want to do something important with their lives—I know I did. I wanted to write the next fantasy epic like Tolkien did. Maybe we're not all cut out for greatness, but that doesn't mean you won't do something great—something crucial, fulfilling, and meaningful.

What I encourage you to do is this: Explore. Take a journey, and don't be afraid of failure. The average person will have eight different careers in their lifetime. Life will take you strange places, and no matter the career you settle on, remember that unexpected detours are necessary, dead ends take you in new directions, and that no job is perfect. There will always be Mondays.

Happy travels.

There and Back Again

When I was young, my father read *The Hobbit* aloud to me. It sparked something, a sense of adventure that said to me a small person in a big world could make a difference. I saw on the book jacket that Tolkien taught at Oxford University in England. While attending Mercer University, I got the opportunity to realize a life-long dream—to study at Oxford for six months on a study abroad program. It meant something for me to visit Tolkien's grave, pay my respects, and know my own journey was far from over.

After college graduation, I signed a one-year volunteer contract to teach English as a Foreign Language (EFL) at a Thai high school. That meant traveling 9,000 miles away from home, family, my girlfriend, and all the people who speak my language. Three months after meeting my students and getting a handle on both teaching English and learning Thai, my father was diagnosed with terminal liver cancer, given "weeks to months" to live. Come March of the next year, my father was still alive, and I returned home to Georgia to continue my life stateside. Having been to Thailand already and having made lasting friendships, I'm sure I'll be back again. I am currently taking care of my father, working as an intern for Gallopade Publishing, and pursuing my passion for writing.

21st Century Career Pathways INDEX

FOR MIDDLE SCHOOL, HIGH SCHOOL, COLLEGE AND **BEYOND!**

"If you are ready for 'readiness'...for choosing a career pathway... deciding what to do after high school...or for a first job, or raise and promotion - THIS SERIES IS FOR YOU!"

– James Barnard

Job Tracks: 60* Great Careers and How to Get from Where You Are... to Where You Want To Go!

This book is filled with unique and effective approaches for helping students find their career pathway! Featuring 60 careers from today's job market, this book allows young people to hear first-hand from a person with the job: how they got it, what they do, what education and skills were required, and "what I would have done differently!" Readers get the feel of what particular careers might actually be like—essential knowledge for that all-important decision!

"Entertaining and charming to read!"

Essential Skills for the Real World of Work: Things EVERY Student Must Know!

There's no other book that does a better job of sharing essential skills for the real business world and explaining why they are essential! This book dishes out the subtleties, nuances, and in-between-the-lines considerations of job interviewers who are not only interested in candidates with essential skills, but are actually desperate for them! It includes a fun and effective scoring system to encourage students to rack up job-readiness skills long before they are required.

"Highly encouraging and enlightening!"

Would You Hire This Person? A Look at Getting Hired (or Not!)...from the Point of View of Your (Possible!) Future Employer

Read verbatim interviews that are both entertaining and enlightening! In this book, students hear both sides of the interview, including the employer and job candidate's unspoken thoughts. The reader can decide for himself or herself if they would hire the job candidate before learning the actual outcome.

"Such realistic scenarios – I got nervous reading them! I wanted the person to get the job, but, gee...I can see why some would not!"

www.careerscurriculum.com

Work Words: Job/Business/Career Words & Terms You Need to Know!

Get ready for lots of insider information and a few inside jokes! Written by a real employer, this book defines essential job, business, and career words and terms with insight, humor, and pizzazz! The contents of the book are organized into entertaining and effective groupings.

"Why be embarrassed when you can be empowered by knowing 'job speak' BEFORE you even get the job?"

Business Ethics & Etiquette for Students: You MUST Know These!

This highly entertaining and immensely practical book is an eye-opening must-read for students and new hires! It provides them with the confidence to avoid embarrassment, misstep, lost opportunity, and more.

"Fascinating and quite a lot of material covered. Anyone can benefit from this double-whammy of info book!"

The Parent and Teacher's Guide: Helping Students Navigate the Bumpy Road from School to More School, First Job, and Career

Filled with candid help from someone who has traveled the bumpy road of "non-readiness" from school to job to career, this book boasts timely and honest information that will help kids get ready for the real world of work. The wealth of ideas available to parents and teachers in this book will help them to navigate their student's journey ahead!

"Marsh has a keen sense of devotion to every type of student truly seeking a path to success. This book is worth the price for the compassion and humor, explanation of 'Rigor vs. Rigor Mortis,' and 'Why Study These Subjects' section. She's clearly 'been there, done that,' and achieved great success despite many obstacles!"

Carole Marsh's CAREERS CURRICULUM™

PLEASE CONTINUE TO VISIT OUR WEBSITE FOR MORE K-12 PRODUCTS IN PRINT & ONLINE FORMATS, INCLUDING:

- INDIVIDUAL CAREER MANUAL
- SCHOOL INFORMATION SHEETS
- COMPANY PROFILE SHEETS
- MAP OF OPPORTUNITIES
- ESSENTIAL SKILLS PASSPORT BOOK

... AND MUCH MORE!!

FOR MIDDLE SCHOOL, HIGH SCHOOL, COLLEGE AND **BEYOND!**

www.careerscurriculum.com